David Hegg has earned the right
A pastor's son, he now faithfully
As an ordination mentor, he sees
who desire to be effective pastor
is at the same time convicting and inspiring, concise yet
thorough, theological yet practical. The reader will be treated
to a fast-paced exploration of the Scriptures backed by hardball
application of those Scriptures to our practice. Whether you are
considering the pastorate, are already a pastor, or are leading
pastors, the benefits of David's work will far outweigh the brief
investment of time it takes to read it.

Steve Highfill,
District Superintendent, Southwest District,
Evangelical Free Church of America

There once was a day in America when an ordained minister
was called 'The Parson'. He was the one person in the
community who was best prepared, most trusted and admired.
That day has ended. He is now referred to as 'The C.E.O.', 'the
Spiritual Mentor' and 'The Motivator'. This shift is eroding the
very integrity of the pastorate. The ministry is not for eager
volunteers attempting to help God out of an overwhelming
plan or for those feeling this would be a nice professional 'fit'.
If the faithful proclamation of God's Message is to be valued
above today's mass media, if the spiritual health of the church
is to be treasured above interpreting marketing trends, if the
integrity of a leader is to be required above personal charisma
and if these things are the highest priorities of God, then the
requirements and the procedures leading to ordination must be
re-examined. David Hegg's book, *Appointed to Preach*, is a book
long overdue. It should be in the hands of every person seeking
ordination as well as local church leaders and denominational
ordination councils. His thoughtful and thorough exploration
lifts the pastorate back to a position it once enjoyed. I highly
recommend this book to those who long to see reformation in
the church.

Don Smith,
Christ Community Church, Laguna Hills, California

Here is a unique and timely book. David Hegg has done great service to the church by tackling this matter with biblical clarity and warm pastoral concern. The ease with which it is possible to read this book belies the depth of insight which it contains. As you read it you will want to pause often, turning to the various passages of Scripture and taking time to think through the implications of these most vital truths.

Alistair Begg,
Senior Pastor, Parkside Church, Chagrin Falls, Ohio

Appointed to Preach

Assessing a Call to Ministry

DAVID W. HEGG

MENTOR

David W. Hegg has been in pastoral ministry for 20 years and presently pastors Grace Baptist Church in Santa Clarita, California where he lives with his wife Cherylyn. He holds a D. Min from Westminster Seminary in California and is an adjunct professor at The Master's College. He is the author of *The Obedience Option* and blogs at www.heggthought.com

Copyright © David W. Hegg 1999

ISBN 978-1-84550-619-3

Published in 1999, Reprinted in 2010
in the
Mentor Imprint
by
Christian Focus Publications, Ltd.
Geanies House, Fearn, Ross-shire,
IV20 1TW, Scotland, United Kingdom

Cover design
by
Daniel van Straaten

Printed by
Bell and Bain, Glasgow

Mixed Sources
Product group from well-managed forests and other controlled sources
www.fsc.org Cert no. TT-COC-002769
© 1996 Forest Stewardship Council

CONTENTS

FOREWORD *by Alistair Begg* 7

PROLOGUE 11

PART 1: Introduction 15

Chapter 1
The Appointment of God's Man 17

Chapter 2
The Affirmation of God's People 31

Chapter 3
The Man Whom God Appoints:
    Character and Desire...53

Chapter 4
The Man Whom God Appoints:
    Message and Gifts...75

PART 2: Introduction 91

Chapter 5
The Process of Ordination......................................93

Chapter 6
Preparing for Ordination 107

Chapter 7
The Ordination Council..125

APPENDIX
Gaining Knowledge and Discernment....................141

SCRIPTURE INDEX 155

DEDICATION

This book is dedicated to my father Dr O. H. Hegg. Dad, you were my first and best pastor, and through your life and preaching you passed on to me a legacy of holiness, a love for the Word and a passion to preach. A better inheritance I could never imagine.

Foreword

Here is a unique and timely book. Unlike other subjects, which are the focus of constant discussion and form the content of numerous books, the matter of ordination is largely and sadly neglected. David Hegg has done great service to the church by tackling this matter with biblical clarity and warm pastoral concern. Its timeliness is obvious when we recognize the church's emphasis over the last three decades or so on the rediscovery of the gifts of the Spirit and the priesthood of all believers. At its best, such an emphasis has mobilized local churches for ministry; and, at its worst, it has led to the neglect of the proper place that must be given to the special gift of Christ to His church – that of pastors and teachers. The author is very clear in presenting the biblical emphasis that the call to shepherd God's people and to teach them His Word is a special calling. It is also a specific calling, in so far as the individual is, according to Hegg, 'appointed to preach'. And it is a strategic calling in the light of the unique importance which it possesses for the spiritual well-being of Christ's flock.

David Hegg has done us a great service by gathering material in a manner not dissimilar to an earlier era, but without any of the accompanying stodginess or archaic language. In a lucid and refreshing style he unearths for the contemporary reader material that one previously had to search around for in the works of Thornwell or Spurgeon. It is clear throughout that this is not the work of a bystander choosing to comment on the need of the hour. Rather it is passionate in its concern, coming as it does from the heart of one who has been called into the very fray of gospel ministry, and who rejoices in being shut up to that call.

This book will be of help to many on a number of fronts. First of all, to the local church, in considering those to whom it should or should not give encouragement in relationship to their sensing a call to pastoral ministry. There is no doubt that many of our seminaries have people in them who would have been helpfully prevented from attendance if their local church had understood correctly the matters that are raised in this book. Every eldership should read this in the course of their meetings until they have fastened onto its truth and are committed to its application. At the same time, every young man who senses within him the stirring of a desire for pastoral ministry will benefit tremendously from reading this book carefully and prayerfully. David is in no doubt that the familiar adage is to be heeded carefully, 'If you can avoid entering the ministry, do so! If you can do something else, do it!' It is also going to be a great boon to ordination councils and seminary faculties as they seek to take seriously the privileged responsibility of seeing young men prepared for pastoral ministry.

The ease with which it is possible to read this book belies the depth of insight that it contains. As you read it you will want to pause often, turning to the various passages of Scripture and taking time to think through the implications of these most vital truths. You will also find that it stirs your heart to pray with renewed vigour that at a time when preaching is in the shadows, the Lord might be pleased to raise up men such as those envisaged in this book. Men like John the Baptist, to whom the Word of God came, and as a result engaged in a Bible-based, Christ-focused, self-effacing ministry of proclamation. May God use this book to that end in each of our lives. I commend it warmly to you.

Alistair Begg,
Senior Pastor, Parkside Church, Chagrin Falls, Ohio

Prologue

As the son of a minister, I knew the one thing I didn't want to be when I grew up was a preacher. Even though I loved my dad, and thought he was really great at what he did, I dreamed of being an attorney, a physician, an athlete, a teacher ... anything but a man who spent his hours studying the Bible and telling people how to live. But somewhere during those college days filled with sports, classes, papers, musical tours and Cherylyn, God drafted me and put his appointment on my life. I didn't fully understand it at the time; neither did I enjoy those first thoughts about devoting my life to the preaching of his Word. Looking back I see now that God first drafted me, and then put me through a customized boot camp specifically designed to fit me for his service. During my personal ten-year 'basic training', He not only changed my heart, but shattered my definition of success and reformed my whole understanding of life in Christ. And while I am not suggesting that everyone entering the preaching ministry needs to repeat my experiences, my years of pastoral ministry have confirmed this conviction: *when God calls a man to pastoral ministry, he also fits that man with the necessary character, desire, knowledge, and ministerial gifts to do the tasks assigned.*

As a local church pastor it has been my privilege to sit on numerous ordination councils examining men determined to enter the preaching ministry. I wish I could say this has always been a pleasant and encouraging experience. But, sadly, far too many men entering pastoral ministry today have great deficiencies in character, biblical knowledge, theological understanding, and ministerial gifts. Often they seem academically lazy, their biblical and theological knowledge is superficial, and they can't preach their way out of the proverbial paper bag. Years of serving on a Credentialing Council of the Evangelical Free Church of America (Southwest District), combined with the work done preparing this book, have brought me to a second fundamental conviction that serves as a corollary to the one stated above. *When God fits a man with the necessary character, desire, knowledge, and ministerial gifts for pastoral ministry, these essentials will clearly be both identifiable and, when measured by Scriptural standards, commendable.*

Throughout the history of the church, men who desired to enter pastoral ministry have been examined to see if their desire was a result of God's divine appointment on their life. While it differs slightly from one ecclesiastical community to the next, this process of ordination has acted to help the church in two ways. First, it has helped the church by protecting it from those who were unqualified to lead and feed the church, even as it maintained the value and honor of the pastoral office. Secondly, by affirming his divine call, it has given the ordained minister the boldness to be God's man while holding him strictly accountable to proclaim God's message and live up to God's standards. Where ordination was held in high esteem, and the expectations placed on candidates were great, the church benefited tremendously. But today all too often ordination has been drastically down-sized in the mind of both candidate and church. While there are some notable exceptions, many denominations today confer ordination on men whose lives they really do not know well, whose knowledge of the Bible and theology demonstrates no depth of thought or breadth of understanding, and whose abilities to communicate God's Word and counsel His people are either unknown or sadly lacking.

My purpose in writing this book is not that I think I can change the world, or even that I think solving the problems I see in ordination councils will put everything right and usher in revival. I merely want to encourage those involved with pastoral ministry to re-think the area of ordination, and I offer a philosophy and model of ordination that, if put into practice in some manner, I believe will help our churches one at a time, one man at a time, to the glory of God.

If the ministry of the Word to God's people has always been a priority in God's plan, if the health of the church depends upon being nourished by the truth of God's Word, and if God has promised that He will give gifted pastors and teachers to the church for her well-being and the expansion of His kingdom on earth, then we ought to care deeply about who these men are, how they live, and what they know of God. In short, since it is in our best interest as the church to identify God's divinely appointed pastors, ordination matters. It matters to the church; it matters to the candidates; and it matters to God.

PART 1

Introduction

Before we can understand why ordination matters, we must first understand what ordination is, and how it works generally. Ordination consists of two parts. The first part has to do with the personal appointment of a man by God Himself. This is often referred to as 'the call of God' on a man's life. In chapter 1 we will look broadly at this side of the ordination process. In chapter 2 we will see the second necessary half of ordination: the affirmation by the church of the man who claims to have been personally appointed by God. In chapters 3 and 4 we will see the distinguishing marks that the church must look for in recognizing and affirming a man for ordained ministry.

Part 1

Introduction

1

The Appointment of God's Man

I can still remember the missionary speaker 'sounding the call' at Lost Lake Bible Camp during my junior high years in Washington state. Missionary hour was one of the staples of our camp experience every morning, and I along with my buddies saw it as one more thing to endure until we could finally hit the softball field. But one year the missionary speaker was better than most; in fact, he was really good! I was especially excited about the snake skins, and turtle shells, and witch doctor stuff he hauled around in his black leather bag. These 'curios' certainly increased my curiosity, and my attention span. But what still stands out in my mind was his closing statement every morning: 'God is looking for volunteers! He needs you to be a missionary, to be a pastor, to work for Him. God is looking for volunteers.' But is He?

When it comes to putting men into pastoral ministry, the evidence shows that God drafts those He intends to use in leadership. Far from calling for volunteers, God descended upon Moses, upon the prophets, the disciples, Paul, and a host of other men down through history. The idea that God is waiting for men to come to him and sign on as leaders in His kingdom may appeal to our modern sense of nobility, but it just won't stand up to the evidence of Scripture.

The Old Testament
In Exodus the story of Moses dominates the landscape. Reading about the miraculous deliverance of the infant

from the river into the household of the Pharaoh's daughter drives home the point that this life is being managed by God Himself. By chapter 3 an adult Moses is ready to be confronted with the life task God has in mind for him. Having heard the cry of His people in bondage (v. 9), God has determined to send Moses (v. 10) to deliver them from Egypt. But Moses is reluctant. In fact, over the next two chapters Moses balks at God's appointment four times, and four times God overrules him. Moses objects that he is a nobody, that he can't possibly convince the people, that they surely won't believe that God spoke to him from a bush, and on top of it all, he doesn't speak very well! But God counters: *I will be with you, and you can tell them I AM sent you. I will give you the ability to do the miraculous as proof of your divine appointment. I, the one who made your lips and tongue, will be with your mouth and teach you what you are to say!*

But even that wasn't enough for Moses. A fifth time he tried to get God to choose someone else, and that caused the anger of God to burn against him. But God had chosen this man, and so He brought Moses' brother Aaron into the picture to serve as spokesman.

God wanted Moses, and not even his reluctance and lack of ability mattered. God could, and did, fit Moses for the ministry.

When Moses died, God went after Joshua. Numbers 27:12-23 gives the poignant picture of God telling Moses of his impending death. Moses, understanding the perilous situation this would create in Israel, immediately implores God to raise up another shepherd for them. He calls on God in verses 15-17:

> Then Moses spoke to the LORD, saying, 'May the LORD, the God of the spirits of all flesh, appoint a man over the congregation, who will go out and come in before them, and who will lead them out and bring them in, that the

congregation of the LORD may not be like sheep which have no shepherd.'

The text goes on to reveal that God already had such a shepherd in mind: Joshua, 'a man in whom is the Spirit' (v. 18). Joshua 1:1-9 recounts God's charge to him and serves as his appointment address. Again we see that God, having chosen Joshua, now moves to fit him for the task, as described in Joshua 1:5:

> No man will be able to stand before you all the days of your life. Just as I have been with Moses, I will be with you; I will not fail you or forsake you.

The stories of the prophets reveal God as the initiator as well. While not every prophet's call to ministry is reported, those described are far from volunteerism.

In Isaiah 6:9 we read of the prophet's appointment to 'go and tell the people' the message God entrusted to him. And many have used this text to suggest that God is seeking volunteers when He asks, 'Whom shall I send, and who will go for Us?' But the context is quite clear that Isaiah's answer to God's call was not that of a volunteer, but that of a man whose life had been fitted already by the very One calling him to service. First God chose Isaiah, and in so doing, ruined him (Isa. 6:1-5). Then He demonstrated through the symbolic purification of the fiery coal that He would prepare Isaiah for the task He had assigned him (Isa. 6:6). It was after the promise that Isaiah's life would be purified, and his iniquity taken away that he was able to respond, 'Here am I. Send me.'

In the case of Jeremiah, we see the same central truths. First, God says, 'Before I formed you in the womb I knew you, and before you were born I consecrated you; I have appointed you a prophet to the nations' (Jer. 1:5), to which Jeremiah responds, 'Alas, Lord GOD! Behold I do not know how to speak, because I am a youth' (Jer. 1:6).

But as with Moses, God is not put off. 'Do not say "I am a youth", because everywhere I send you, you shall go, and all that I command you, you shall speak' (Jer. 1:7). Later in the chapter, God insists that He has put His words in the prophet's mouth, a consistent metaphor for the entrusting of a specific message to the prophet (Jer. 1:9), and promises to give the young man the personal fortitude necessary to proclaim the truth to people who will rebel and even fight against it (Jer. 1:17-19). In Jeremiah, as with the others, we find a reluctant man, aware of his grave shortcomings, drafted by God with a promise that he would fit him with both the character and the message necessary to get God's job done.

Ezekiel's story continues the same theme. Over the course of the first three chapters of his prophecy, Ezekiel gives a first hand account of his call to ministry. In every situation, God himself initiates the relationship. God comes to Ezekiel in several visions, each specifically designed to instruct the prophet in the way he should act as God's spokesman. Again, the theme is that God overwhelms the man, and then stands him up, instructs him, and fortifies him to carry out his orders.

We can't conclude this overview of the Old Testament without looking at Jonah, the most reluctant of all ambassadors. Of all the minor prophets, only Jonah's story includes his call to ministry, and what a story it is. Jonah 1:2 gives us the succinct charge God brought to the man: 'Arise, go to Nineveh that great city, and cry against it, for their wickedness has come up before me.' Later, in Jonah 3:2, God spoke to him a second time telling him to 'proclaim to it [the city] the proclamation which I am going to tell you'. God knew Jonah's deficiencies. Like every other man, he needed God's message and God intended to give it to him lest he be left to his own creative devices. But we all know how Jonah responded.

He ran, and dived, and made a big splash! But God had chosen him, and his desertion was merely a radical part of God's plan to fit Jonah with the character and attitude He would use to bring revival to Nineveh. And that is the real story of Jonah. The biggest miracle in the book is not at all the fact that Jonah survived his three days of forced accommodation in the belly of the fish. The great miracle was that a city of 120,000 people repented in sackcloth before God, 'from the least even to the greatest' (Jonah 3:5) through the preaching of a simple, God-given message delivered by a less than perfect human spokesman.

From these stories of Old Testament men it is clear that God comes to a man, and drafts him, often before the man thinks he is ready. God moves on the man's heart, turning it toward him and in so doing often produces a reluctance borne of humility and personal inadequacy. And who doesn't find himself in over his head when called of God to deliver His message his way? But the God who calls is the God who enables, and in every case, where he appoints a man, he also fits and furnishes him.

Before moving on to the New Testament it is important to see the significance all this has for the process of ordination today. It is just this: *the way you view the call of God on the life of a man will determine the manner in which you go about affirming that call.*

If God is putting the need before us, and is waiting for volunteers to take on leadership through pastoral ministry, then ordination will be seen as a process to help as many men as possible enter that ministry. And while it may continue to take on a role of examination, it will certainly not be allowed to keep sincere, faithful men out of public ministry. After all, we need them! Consequently, standards will be adjusted to accommodate more and more men, even if this means lessening the requirements and lowering the expectations. If this is done out of a sincere motive to broaden the influence of the kingdom by increasing the number of laborers, it is laudable. And yet, even sincere motives cannot overcome the consequences of improper thinking regarding ordination. The fact is we do not just need more men; we need the men God has truly called and gifted for pastoring and preaching.

What the church lacks today is not quantity but quality in her pulpits. A strong case can be made that we presently have too many men in pastoral ministry; too many who have taken the mantle of leadership upon themselves without having been selected and formed by God for that purpose. They preach, but not with power and often not with truth; they lead, but not from the platform of a life of godliness, holiness, and prayer; and slowly these men are changing the face of pastoral leadership. What once was a ministry of humble dependence upon God and his Word is more and more becoming a position of power and influence dependent upon marketing strategies, programming innovations, and an increasing infatuation with technology and culture. The image of a pastor as a servant-teacher is fast being replaced with that of a Chief Executive Officer whose knowledge of modern organizational theory and communication technique is more highly prized than his commitment to praying and preaching. The church needs to protect itself against such as these, and a fresh look at the process of ordination will help.

If, as seems clear from the Old Testament stories cited, God initiates the call and appoints men to ministry, then the process whereby the church critiques and affirms this divine call in the life of a man takes on great significance. Ordination thus becomes the means to limit pastoral ministry to those upon whom God has clearly placed His hands in appointing them especially to His work. It serves as a sort of scanner, not unlike those used to screen passengers in airports. But in the case of ordination its job is to affirm the presence of certain things as well as make sure certain things are not found. Those whom God has drafted and appointed will be identified by the presence of certain character qualities, a righteous and commendable attitude regarding servant leadership, thorough knowledge of God's Word, a consistent and comprehensive theological viewpoint, and evident ministerial gifts. When a man with these qualities is examined, the ordination scanner recognizes that the call on his life, expressed in his desire to enter pastoral ministry, is indeed of God. Others are found to be wanting, and the church will benefit by their exclusion. In this view of the call to ministry, ordination plays a very important role. Because it serves the church in such a vital area, its standards must not be lowered. Imagine turning down the sensitivity dial on the airport scanner just so more people could bring bigger metal objects on the plane. Rather, the standards must be held high and proclaimed loudly. As we will see in later chapters, a high view of ordination, and the great expectations that come with it, will serve both the candidate and the church greatly by honoring and affirming the great value of the pastoral office while protecting the church from those who would misuse or abuse it.

The New Testament

In his book *The Preacher's Portrait*, John R. W. Stott, in describing the New Testament preacher and his task, uses five images: Steward, Herald, Witness, Father, and Servant.[1]

While all of these certainly speak to the varied ways the New Testament minister lives and functions, it is the image of *herald* that speaks most powerfully to our subject. In fact, the concept of herald incorporates most

---

1   John R. W. Stott, *The Preacher's Portrait*, Eerdmans, 1961, p. 9.

of the others, for the herald of that day was indeed a steward entrusted with a message that he had himself witnessed. And certainly, as a member of the king's court, he was to perform all of his duties as a servant of his master. Looking more closely at the New Testament image of the herald will help define God's appointment of men to the work of pastoring today.

In the New Testament the concept of the pastor as 'herald' is drawn from the New Testament use of the word *khrux*. The *khrux* word group includes the noun: *khrux* (*kērux*, herald, one who proclaims); the verb: *khrussw* (*kērussō*, to herald, to proclaim); and the noun: *khrugma* (*kērugma*, the proclamation, the message heralded). The word group was well known, and widely used in the Greek world. The noun form is found some ninety times in Homer alone.[2] As a result, it is possible to get a clear understanding of the position, honor, and authority which the herald enjoyed.

It is clear that the herald occupied a definite position in the royal court. Each sovereign had his spokesman, his herald. In Acts 14, when Paul and Barnabas were in Lystra, the people responded to the healing of the lame man with shouts proclaiming Barnabas to be Zeus, and Paul to be his spokesman Hermes, because '[Paul] was the chief speaker'. Knowing that every king had his human mouthpiece, they ascribed such a relationship to Barnabas and Paul.

According to Friedrich, '[the herald] had a place at the royal court. Every prince had a herald, in some cases several. To him was ascribed both political and religious significance. He was very highly regarded.'[3]

---

2   Gerhard Friedrich, '*khrux*, (i.e. *rokhrux*), *khrussw, khrugma, prokhrussw*,' in Theological Dictionary of the New Testament, ed. Gerhard Friedrich and Gerhard Kittel, 10 vols. (rand Rapids: Eerdmans, 1964-1976), 3:683, note 3.

3   Friedrich, 'khrux,' pp. 683, 684.

Of the qualities required of the herald, two were primary. First, he had to have a good voice. As it was his job to speak to large groups on behalf of the king, or to summon townspeople to specific actions or meetings, it was necessary that he have the vocal ability to do so. Secondly, and perhaps more importantly, the herald had to possess certain character qualities. As the requirement of a good voice assured his ability to do the job, the character of the herald assured that the integrity of the message would be preserved. Given the authority entrusted to the herald and the potential damage which could arise from exaggerated or compromised messages, it was absolutely necessary that such a one be a man of character who could be trusted to deliver the message as it had been delivered to him. As Friedrich further explains:

> The essential point about the report which they give is that it does not originate with them. Behind it stands a higher power. The herald does not express his own views. He is the spokesman for his master.... Heralds adopt the mind of those who commission them, and act with the plenipotentiary authority of their masters.... It is unusual for a herald to act on his own initiative and without explicit instructions. In the main the herald simply gives short messages, puts questions, and brings answers.... In rare cases he may be empowered to decide on his own. But in general he is simply an executive instrument. Being only the mouth of his master, he must not falsify the message entrusted to him by additions of his own. He must deliver it exactly as given to him.... In the assembly and in court he is the voice of the chairman, and in other aspects of his work as well he must keep strictly to the words and orders of his master. [4]

While in the Greek world the khrux (*kērux*) held a prominent position, when we turn to the New Testament we find

---

4   Friedrich, 'khrux,' p. 688.

that the person of the herald is not nearly as dominant as
the message which is delivered. The noun *khrux* (khrux) is
found only three times in the New Testament. It is *khrussw*
(khrussw), the act of proclaiming, which dominates the New
Testament description of the work of the herald. However,
it must not be assumed that the lack of use necessarily
diminishes the sense that the New Testament preacher did,
in fact, occupy a position of herald for the living God.

The three uses of the noun *khrux* (*kērux*) are all found
in the later writings of the New Testament. Twice Paul
uses the term to describe the position to which he was
appointed (1 Tim. 2:7; 2 Tim. 1:11), and Peter uses the
term to describe Noah (2 Pet. 2:5). It is Paul's use of
the term that offers insight into the significance of the
position of herald for today.

The Pastoral Epistles were written near the end of
Paul's ministry. In them he exhorts Timothy and Titus
to take the ministry entrusted to him, and continue it.
Specifically, he exhorts them in the tasks of maintaining
blameless character, and preserving and proclaiming the
Word. While not specifically calling Timothy and Titus
a *khrux* (khrux), Paul does demand of them all those
things associated with the position:

Character:	1 Timothy 3:1-13, 15; 4:12, 16; 6:11; 2 Timothy 2:19-22; Titus 1:5-9; 2:11-14
Guard the Truth:	1 Timothy 1:3-5, 18-20; 4:7, 14; 5:21; 6:12-14; 2 Timothy 1:13, 14; 2:15; 3:14-16; 4:15
Preach the Truth:	1 Timothy 1:3; 4:6, 11, 13, 16; 6:17, 18; 2 Timothy 1:6; 2:24-26; 4:1-5

Paul, in passing along the torch of proclamation to Timothy, charges him to 'herald the Word' (2 Tim. 4:2). This charge, given 'in the presence of God and of Christ Jesus' certainly underscores the gravity of Timothy's appointment and sets the standard for acceptable performance of the duties that came with being God's herald.

As mentioned above, Paul and other New Testament writers seemed to be much more interested in the act of proclamation than in the position. *khrussw* (*kērussō*) **is used some sixty times in the New Testament. Associated as this word was to the position of** *khrux* (*kērux*) its broad use in the New Testament does suggest that the task of faithfully proclaiming an entrusted message was both widely known and well respected. Forms of *khrussw* (*kērussō*) are used to describe the activity of John the Baptist (Mark 1:4); as well as that of Jesus (Mark 1:14). In Mark 1:38 Jesus boldly states that his primary task during the Galilean ministry was to 'preach' (*khruxw, kēruxō*). Philip is described as 'proclaiming' (*ejkhrussen, ekērussen*) Christ. Throughout the remainder of the New Testament the word group is used to describe the authoritative proclamation of the message concerning Christ. This task is perhaps best described in Paul's strong charge to Timothy in 2 Timothy 4:1-5, which will be considered in detail in later chapters.

This authoritative type of proclamation is well defined in the New Testament. First, the message delivered (*khrugma, kērugma*) is never used of a written message. Paul does not charge either Timothy or Titus to take up a writing ministry. He only encourages them in the areas of teaching (*didaskw, didaskō*) and preaching (*khrussw, kērussō*). Neither is this word group descriptive of the responsibility of every Christian to spread the good news. This general task of 'gossiping the gospel' is usually described by *eujaggelizomai* (*euangelizomai*, e.g. see Acts 8:4).

But perhaps the most defining characteristic of *khrussw* (*kērussō*) is that it is always associated with an appointed spokesman, one who speaks that which has been entrusted to him. In this speaking, he speaks with the full authority of the one whose message he speaks, and his audience is to respond to the message just as if the originator of the message were speaking directly to them. Paul tells Timothy that his (Paul's) position as *khrux* (*kērux*) came by divine appointment; it was not a position which he took upon himself (2 Tim. 1:11). While Timothy is nowhere referred to as *khrux* (*kērux*), the requirements put upon him, coupled with the official appointment (see 1 Tim. 4:14; 2 Tim. 1:6) conferred upon him, suggest that his preaching task was one of being a herald, entrusted with an authoritative message from God, as we will see.

Perhaps the clearest text describing the preacher as *khrux* (*kērux*) is Romans 10:14,15:

> How then shall they call upon him in whom they have not believed? And how shall they believe in him whom they have not heard? And how shall they hear without a preacher? And how shall they preach unless they are sent?

In this text Paul lays out the place and task of the herald-preacher. First, the decision of faith (calling on the Name of the Lord) is dependent upon believing the message of the gospel. Further, belief is dependent upon hearing the gospel message. But the gospel message can only be heard as it is proclaimed by a preacher (here *khrussonto"*, *khrussontos*). And yet the preacher can only go out and proclaim the message authoritatively as he is sent! Here we have all the pieces. The *khrux* (*kērux*) is a man under orders, appointed by his superior to deliver a message. It is his faithful proclamation of this message, apart from compromise, that is the means by which those who hear may be savingly set upon by God unto salvation. Thus the herald-preacher has a three-fold responsibility:

1) To be faithful to the one by whom he has been appointed by keeping his character blameless and above reproach (see 1 Tim. 3:1ff);

2) To be faithful in delivering the message as it has been entrusted to him being careful to tell the truth, the whole truth, and nothing but the truth; and

3) To be faithful in going out to the audience for whom the message proclaimed is the only hope of eternal salvation.

William Hendricksen summarized it this way: 'According to Scripture, then, "heralding" or "preaching" is generally the divinely authorized proclamation of the message of God to men. It is the exercise of ambassadorship.'[5]

To the examples cited above may be added another interesting herald in the New Testament. In Luke 1 and 2 the angelic messenger Gabriel is sent from God on two different missions. What is interesting is that, when Zechariah questions God's message, Gabriel responds to him (Luke 1:19) with this clear declaration of the position and purpose of the herald:

> And the angel answered and said to him, 'I am Gabriel, who stands in the presence of God; and I have been sent to speak to you, and to bring you good news.'

While the *khrux* (khrux) word group is not used specifically, this text does give insight into the self-concept of God's messengers: they get their message from God, and they are sent by God to proclaim that message without any addition or deletion. And if we fast forward to the last of Gabriel's three missions, to the shepherds on

---

5   William Hendricksen; *New Testament Commentary, Exposition of The Pastoral Epistles*; Baker Book House, p. 309 (italics in the original).

Christmas Eve, we see another important element in the life of the herald. After hearing the words of the angelic messenger (Luke 2:10-12), notice what the shepherds say among themselves: 'Let us go straight to Bethlehem then, and see this thing that has happened, *just as the Lord has made known to us*' (italics mine). Don't miss this point! The success of the messenger, the herald, is that after the message is delivered, the audience remembers it, not merely as the sound of the messenger, but as the message of the Lord.

So far we have seen, both from the Old and New Testaments, that God uses men of His choosing to lead His people through the faithful proclamation of His Word. Little has been said about this call on the individual because, in truth, so little is said about it in Scripture. That God calls men is true; that this call grows from a spark to a fire of desire for ministry is in agreement with Paul's statement in 1 Timothy 3:1 that such a desire is a good thing. But just what constitutes this desire? How is divinely produced desire for ministry distinguished from what Charles Bridges calls 'self-deceiving presumption' on the part of a man who seeks to enter the preaching office for reasons other than God's appointment?[6] A proper philosophy and process of ordination is dependent upon understanding that God's appointment of a man will be made evident by the way the man is distinctively fitted by God for the task assigned. When the desire for ministry is of God, certain things will be clearly seen in the man. And while the presence of some or all of the characteristics of divine appointment do not always guarantee that the man has been appointed by God, where these things are lacking it must be determined that the man has not been drafted by God to be His herald.

---

6   Charles Bridges, *The Christian Ministry* (reprint of 1830 ed., Banner of Truth, 1967), pp. 100-101.

2

The Affirmation of God's People

One Sunday following our preaching services, I was standing at the entrance to our auditorium greeting folks as they made their way out on a bright, sunny California morning. As I shook the hands of one new couple, the husband told me that he too was a preacher and that God had told him to come to our town to start a church. In response to my questions about his plan, he explained that though he had no academic training, and no official connection with any church or denomination, he knew beyond any doubt that God had called him not only to preach, but to start a church in our part of the city. I can remember praying silently, 'Lord, what do I say to this man? How can I discourage him in an encouraging way?' As I began to explain my view of ministry and the importance of making sure of God's call, it became clear that his mind was made up. Like so many others in our day, he was a captive of an *individualized* concept of Christian living in which the *personal experiences of the individual outweigh and finally eclipse the revelatory and corporate dimensions of Biblical Christianity.* What he believed was based on personal experience and formed the foundation of his life plan, and left little, if any, room for what Scripture taught on the subject, or what the Church has historically practised.

Sadly, I don't know what happened to that man for he never returned, even though I offered to help him. But I have seen many other men take the same path he was walking. It appears that, once again, the fingers of our modern culture have wrapped themselves around the heart of the church. Just like the unbelieving world, we are increasingly tempted as individuals to 'pull our own strings', 'look out for number 1' and make our personal dreams our reality despite what others may think. We prize the dream of the individual above the wisdom of the group. And nowhere is this more damaging to the church than in the case of men entering ministry on their own, apart from the affirmation of the church. In chapter 1 we saw that when God drafts a man, He is also faithful to craft and fit that man for ministry. In this chapter we will see that when God calls a man to ministry, He extends the right to exercise the prerogatives of that ministry through the affirmation of the church. The internal call of God to the man is not enough; it must be activated for use in public ministry by the external call of God through the church. As we will see, not only is this of great benefit to the man himself, but it is a very necessary protection to the church.

The Sphere of Ordination

Before describing the role of the church in affirming God's appointment of a man, it will help first to define the areas of ministry for which ordination ought to be required.

Not long ago I was approached by a man who worked in the marketing department of what is often referred to as a 'para-church' Christian ministry organization. He told me he was in charge of brochures, advertising, and client development. When he heard of my interest in the concept of ordination, he immediately explained that he was thinking of pursuing ordination. My confusion must have registered on my face, for he quickly began arguing that, while he was in marketing, he believed that he was called to marketing by God and that he was a minister of the gospel, though in an alternative setting. As he explained further I got a clearer sense of his view of ordination, and of ministry. He told me that his goal was to be a director of the organization, or one like it, and that most other directors in his industry were ordained. Ordination, he explained, seemed to give the final stamp of approval needed to gain the highest levels in his field.

But is this the purpose of ordination? Has it become nothing more than the religious world's way of giving added certification to certain of its leaders, similar to what a banker might get by attending a series of classes or seminars? And just who should be ordained? What about para-church leaders, Christian educators, or missionary aviators? Is ordination available and necessary for any and every Christian who involves himself in any type of public ministry?

When addressing the subject of ordination it is helpful first to narrow the scope of study. It is clear from the New Testament that local church elders are to be recognized and officially appointed (Acts 14:23). Likewise, the fact that qualifications are listed for deacons (1 Tim. 3:8-13) suggests that these were to be officially recognized and appointed as well. Further, it is common in some denominations to recognize educators and administrators in seminaries, colleges and other ministry organizations as official ministers through ordination. While all of these raise certain questions that bear on the topic of ordination, they fall outside the focus of this study. In this book the discussion of ordination is focused narrowly on the church's recognition and affirmation of a man's appointment by God to be his herald in the church. I refer to this using a number of phrases including pastoral ministry, preaching ministry, and the exercise of the pastoral office.

Of interest to our discussion of ordination is the way in which pastors, as undershepherds, operate under

Christ in the world. That they are to lead the church is clear from the terms used to designate them in the New Testament.[1] Through the faithful ministry of these men Christ extends His ministry as Prophet, Priest, and King. Through them He speaks forth His truth to His people as they declare the truth of Scripture; through them He is acknowledged to be the great high priest as they intercede for the flock, and lead in prayer; and through them He exercises His kingly rule over His people as they demonstrate servant-leadership and carry out discipline among the flock of God. Because they act as Christ's representatives in the church, and since they have been granted authority over the lives of those in the church, ordination is necessary. To these men has been given the privilege of preaching, praying, leading, and correcting God's household as undershepherds of Christ. And it must be understood that it is God Himself who calls them and grants them this privilege. When the church takes great care to put in positions of leadership only those men whom God Himself has called and given to the church (Eph. 4:11-13), the health of the church is enhanced and its testimony protected.

Consequently, the ordination of men who do not serve as leaders in local churches can lead to a blurring of the distinctiveness of ordination. Where ordination is no longer joined to the work of preaching, praying, leading and correcting, it risks becoming nothing more than a professional achievement. This will raise some necessary questions regarding the ordination of non-church related personnel. But whatever decision is made regarding the scope of ordination in various

---

1   A simple survey of the New Testament shows that the three terms used
     to describe the position of leadership in the church are all used inter-
     changeably for the same office. The Greek terms translated 'bishop',
     'elder', and 'pastor' are found in some form in the following passages,
     and all refer to the same office: Acts 20:17-28; 1 Pet. 5:1, 2.

denominations, we cannot afford to let ordination slip to the level of mere professional certification. Too often men are pursuing ordination, not because they believe they have been appointed by God to serve in the ministry of preaching, praying, leading, and correcting in the church, but in order to gain a type of spiritual certification so as to legitimize their individual ministry or broaden their career opportunities.

The Role of the Church in Ordination

God, who drafts men and fits them for ministry, intends that His work in them be on display so brightly that the church is able to see it, and then able to confirm His call through their appointment to public ministry. These two sides of the ordination coin must never be separated: God works directly on the heart and life of the man in appointing him to ministry, and He works corporately through the church to appoint that man to the public exercise of ministry. It is my contention that the two parts must go together. While the first is necessary, it is not sufficient. The personal experience of the man must be affirmed by the church if that man's ministry is to be seen as sourced in God's divine appointment.

Having said this, it must not be thought that the church is the source of the authority for pastoral ministry. This is a common misconception. We must never forget that the authority for ministry comes from Christ alone. The church only confirms that the necessary external evidence exists to affirm the reality of the individual's internal and personal appointment by God. Bannerman is most helpful in describing this:

> In short, ordination by the Church was the ordinary and authorized method in the apostolic practice for the investiture with office of those found qualified by the previous call and special gifts conferred by Christ. Not

that the ordination by the Church conferred a right to the office of the ministry. That right was previously conferred by Christ; and ordination, in itself, was no more than the Church's recognition of the right so conferred, and the Church's admission of the individual to the discharge of the office to which he was thus called.[2]

Biblical Examples

While there are no specific descriptions of ordination processes in the Scripture, there are many examples of the fundamental concept that God works through the church to affirm those He has appointed to pastoral ministry.

The example of Paul is helpful even though, as an apostle, his ministry went beyond what we know today of local church leadership. Given that Paul's 'call' can never be seen as a normative model for today, yet it can be seen that the fundamental principles of ordination are exhibited in his life as he moved from the road to Damascus to a role as church leader in Antioch.

First, it is clear that despite a direct confrontation with the risen Christ and the clear and personal nature of Paul's charge from Christ, he did not immediately enter widespread public ministry to the Gentile peoples. His first attempts to preach Christ were met with such hostility on the part of the Jews that the brethren sent him away to Tarsus. It is widely held that the next three years of his life were spent re-examining his life and beliefs through the lens of Christ. While he did engage in ministry, it seems that the full and public mission to the Gentiles did not go from bud to flower apart from the recognition and affirmation of the church that his charge and calling were of God.

Paul's own description of events in Galatians 1 and 2 suggests that, after his dramatic conversion and

---

2   James Bannerman, *The Church of Christ* (reprint of 1869 ed. Edinburgh: Banner of Truth, 1974) vol. 1: 432.

appointment by God, he went off to Arabia and Damascus for a period of years. After three years he returned to Jerusalem, to meet Peter. Once again he returned to Syria where, despite some public preaching, he was not well-known to the churches. According to Galatians 2:1, it was fourteen years later that Paul came to Jerusalem and there, after he 'submitted to them the gospel' (v. 2) that he had been preaching, James, John and Peter affirmed Paul and his understanding of the message and extended to him the 'right hand of fellowship' in confirmation of 'the grace that had been given' to Paul (v. 9). While it must be affirmed that Paul's appointment as an apostle came directly from Christ, what we can see here is a rough sketch of ordination. A man, called and appointed by Christ, takes a period of years to develop his character and his message. At some point, he submits himself and his message to the leaders of the church who, after examining him carefully, confer upon him their blessing through the extension of their hands, and so affirm the reality of his appointment to ministry.

Later, in Acts 13, we see another version of the same concept. In this case, the leaders of the church at Antioch are commanded by God to 'set apart for me Barnabas and Saul for the work to which I have called them' (v. 2). While the situation and content of their personal call is not given, it is clear that it was not enough. The Holy Spirit not only called Barnabas and Saul to a specific work, but He activated that call to ministry through the affirmation of the church. Once again, the corporate appointment of the men was publicly signified by the extension of hands from the leaders to those being affirmed (v. 3). It is also important to note that at the end of their missionary journey the two men returned to Antioch, signifying that, while they may have appeared to be on their own, they were actually under the authority of the local church and its leaders. Paul's continued association with the church as the affirming body of Christ in his life is further demonstrated in Acts 15:40 where, after choosing Silas as a new ministry partner, they departed 'being committed by the brethren to the grace of the Lord'. Though Paul was an apostle, he demonstrated a dependence upon the church to affirm corporately what he believed God had called him to do personally.

In the person and work of Timothy we also see evidence of the process by which God separates a man unto the public ministry of the Word. As a young man, Timothy was drafted by Paul to travel with him on various of his missionary journeys. Somewhere along the line it became clear that God had also drafted Timothy to be a herald for Him. Paul encourages Timothy to 'herald' the word (2 Tim. 4:2) in that great final charge of the ageing apostle to the young preacher. And yet this charge is but a reminder of the official affirmation of the church that took place in Timothy's life at some prior time. In 1 Timothy 4:14 Paul reminds Timothy not to 'neglect the spiritual gift within you, which was bestowed upon you through prophetic utterance with the laying on of hands by the presbytery'. While no specific process of ordination can be siphoned out of this text, certain indications can be strongly asserted:

1) The 'gift' spoken of refers in some way to Timothy's authorization to represent God as a spokesman for His truth. Paul has sent Timothy to Ephesus (1 Tim. 1:3) to oversee several areas of church life and particularly, to 'instruct' the church. Paul gives Timothy the necessary material to deal with issues involving women in the church, the appointment of elders and deacons, and dealing with widows, among others. But fundamental to carrying out the tasks assigned to him is the proclamation and protection of the apostolic truth. In 1 Timothy 6

Paul is emphatic that Timothy 'keep the commandment without stain or reproach' (v. 14), that he 'guard what has been entrusted to you' and not run after 'worldly and empty chatter, and the opposing arguments of what is falsely called "knowledge" which some have professed and thus gone astray from the truth' (vv. 20, 21). Unlike the others who have wandered away from it, Timothy is charged with keeping the truth. This responsibility toward the protection and proclamation of the divine message is tied to the presbytery's official affirmation of Timothy.

2) Timothy's authoritative position as a protector and proclaimer of God's truth in the church was affirmed by others who themselves were in positions of church leadership. 1 Timothy 4:14 describes these men as the 'presbytery'. They were themselves officially recognized and appointed elders who, in the exercise of their position, were authorized to recognize him as God's appointee. Just how or when this happened is unknown; but that Timothy's position and authority were not the result of his own desire alone, or even the appointment of Paul, but the decision of a group of men is clearly seen. At some point, Timothy was solemnly set apart unto the public ministry of pastoring by other leaders in the church. And their affirmation of his life and message was publicly demonstrated through the extension of their hands to him. It is important to see that Paul continues to remind Timothy of his official corporate appointment in order to shake him from what appears to be ministerial complacency in 2 Timothy 1:6: 'And for this reason, I remind you to kindle afresh the gift of God which is in you through the laying on of my hands.'

In the person of Timothy, then, we see the essence of the ordination process: the gifts and graces of a man are examined over time by the leaders of the church.

At some point, when the man's desire for ministry, his character, gifts, and knowledge plainly manifest that he has been drafted by God, he is publicly affirmed and authorized to exercise the office of pastoral ministry. This demonstrates the importance not only of the man and his personal fitness for ministry, but also the essential role the church plays in the process of setting men apart unto God to exercise that ministry.

While the primary task of affirming men for pastoral ministry falls to the leaders of the church, there is some evidence that the congregation is also to be involved in the process. Certainly when the qualifications for elders and deacons are considered, it is clear that any examination of a man's life must take into account the opinions of the community in which he lives and ministers. The man's life is opened up for examination before the whole body of believers, and even among those outside the church (1 Tim. 3:7). The nature of the qualifications indicate that the man's life and ministry will be examined unofficially by those with whom he lives, over time, long before he becomes the focus of official examination by the leadership. What people see in a life and know about that life is fundamentally important to any process of leadership development.

In Acts 6:3 the apostles recognized the role of the congregation when they told them to 'select from among you, brethren, seven men of good reputation, full of the Holy Spirit and wisdom, whom we may put in charge of this task'. While the official appointment of the seven men was left to the apostles, the congregation were active partners in the process. Their task was to evaluate the lives of men, and select those who qualified. The role of the congregation is further demonstrated in Acts 14:23 where Luke writes, 'And when they had appointed elders for them in every church, having prayed with fasting, they commended them to the Lord in whom they had believed.' Commenting on this text, and especially the meaning of 'appointed', John Calvin says:

> For Luke relates that presbyters were appointed through the churches by Paul and Barnabas; but at the same time he notes the manner, or means, when he says that it was done by votes – 'presbyters elected by show of hands in every church' he says. Therefore, these two apostles 'created' them, but the whole group, as was the custom of the Greeks in elections, declared whom it wished to have by raising hands.[3]

From these biblical examples the role of the church in the ordination of men is clearly demonstrated. Yet, it is not at all clear just how the process happens. In fact, all that we learn from the Scriptures is that men need to measure up, and the church needs to recognize them as set apart by God before putting them into pastoral ministry. Just how this happens is left open. The remainder of this book takes up the question of how best to ordain men today. In the philosophy of ordination presented, and the model given, every effort is made to ground the suggestions in biblical texts or principles. Yet, it must be clearly stated that *no process* is specifically given in the Bible. This means that the church is free in regard to the details of the process, and even the formality of the process itself. Yet all must recognize that while the process is open for discussion, the evidence is clear concerning the responsibility of the church to protect itself by limiting the pastoral office to those who are truly called of God. Ordination must never become optional. That Paul gave Timothy and Titus guidelines for selecting and appointing leaders (see 1 Tim. 3:1-8; Titus 1:6-9) must mean that God intends the church to examine closely all whom it would choose as

---

3   John Calvin, Institutes of the Christian Religion (edited by John T. McNeil, The Westminster Press; Philadelphia) 2:1,065, 1,066.

its spiritual leaders. And while no official process is laid
out in Scripture, the great responsibility of serving as an
undershepherd of Christ in teaching, praying, leading
and correcting His flock demands our best efforts. For
while God is not dependent upon us in order to raise up
laborers for His harvest, He certainly is worthy of our best
and most diligent efforts in raising up and appointing to
His service the best men we have.

How the Church Functions in Ordination

The biblical evidence shows that the church is not passive
in the appointment of those men called to lead it under
Christ. And yet, neither is the ordination process an elec-
tion! Rather, it is a balanced process of examination and
reflection designed to validate the reality of the candidate's internal call through the affirmation of those he has
been called to lead. While the existing church leadership
is responsible for initiating and facilitating the process,
the insights of the congregation – those among whom
the candidate has lived and ministered – are an essential
component of any effective process. The church, under
the direction of its leadership, functions in two ways:
examination and *affirmation*.

Examination

The role of the church in looking out for men whose lives
give evidence of God's appointment needs to be reclaimed
and reaffirmed in our day. For much too long it has been
left to the man himself to initiate any movement into pastoral ministry. While it is not wrong for a man to make
his desire for ministry known, and so start down the path
of ordination, it is also not wrong for church leaders and
well-instructed congregations to be on the lookout for
those men whose gifts make room for them, and whose
lives give some evidence that God may indeed be putting
them into pastoral ministry. I am often reminded, as I read

biographies of great preachers, that in almost every case the man was first directed to pursue ministry not by his own vision but through the encouragement of a spiritual mentor. That future leaders ought to be recognized and encouraged by present leaders fits well with Paul's charge to Timothy in 2 Timothy 2:2: 'And the things which you have heard from me in the presence of many witnesses, these entrust to faithful men, who will be able to teach others also.' While not every disciple will become a pastoral leader, it would serve the church well for us all to be on the lookout for 'faithful men' whom God may be molding into undershepherds of His flock.

In the great process of ordination, then, the church is to be involved in *examination* of men on two levels. First is the initial examination of men to find those among the faithful who, perhaps, are being called by God and would be benefited by entering into the ordination process. The first step of the process, called Licensure, is that initial time period after a man is found to be of godly character, and during which he is given the opportunity to demonstrate his ministerial gifts and deepen his biblical knowledge and theological insight.[4] Both entrance into this phase of ordination and its successful completion depend upon the close and loving scrutiny by the church of his life and message. After completing his time of Licensure, the man then must sit for formal examination. This second level of examination, carried out by a council of leaders organized for this purpose, represents the broadest and deepest examination of the man's character, ministerial aptitude and giftedness, and knowledge.[5] When a man has been thoroughly examined by the church and its leaders, and it has been acknowledged that his life, his gifts, and his message testify to the reality of God's call

---

4   In chapter 5 I present a detailed description of the process of ordination.

on his life, then the church moves to the *affirmation* stage
of the process.

Affirmation

When a man has been examined and found to be God's
herald, it is the joy of the church and its leaders to
affirm his divine appointment to pastoral ministry. This
affirmation, granting to the man all the authority and
responsibility necessary to the exercise of ministerial
office, constitutes the highest charge the church can give
a man. Consequently, it must be seen as very honorable
and conferred with a great sense of seriousness, given
the spiritual gravity of the pastoral task. And yet, the
appointment of a man to service as an under-shepherd of
Christ is also a cause for great celebration. It represents the
fulfilment of God's promise to supply gifted teachers and
leaders to the church for her continued unity, growth, and
over-all well-being (see Eph. 4:11-16). At one and the same
time a man must be overwhelmed with the solemnity of
the position, and filled with enthusiasm and great joy at
the prospect of laboring in the vineyard of Christ. It is
necessary, therefore, that the affirmation of the church be
done in such a way that the man is both duly warned and
fully encouraged as he enters into the office of preaching
and leading the church.

A strategic part of the affirmation process is the public conferral of ordination, often called a commissioning
service. This public gathering is designed to charge the
man with the formal responsibilities of the ministry, and
to declare to the people that he has been officially recognized as God's minister. Such a service may include spoken charges to the candidate, an exposition by him, the
taking of vows by him regarding his duties as a pastor,
the symbolic appointment of him through the laying on
of hands, and the granting of a certificate of ordination.

The Benefits of Ordination

But is ordination really worthwhile, given all the time and effort required to do it well? That many see ordination as nothing more than bureaucratic hoop-jumping today is a cause for alarm. Sadly, what ought to be a vital and encouraging part of a man's entrance into ministry has, in the minds of many, simply become a nuisance, a waste of time that could be better spent in actual ministry to people. Some have even gone so far as to be anti-ordination, and boast of their having been commissioned directly by God quite apart from any human agency.

But is ordination really an obstacle to effective ministry? Is it a waste of a man's time? Is it nothing more than a bureaucratic hurdle, whose time and effectiveness have come and gone? It is time to re-consider the benefits of ordination, both to the minister, and to the church.

Benefits for the Minister

The benefits of ordination to the minister can be summarized in three areas:

1) *Assurance*: Anyone who serves in pastoral leadership soon finds out that the waters of ministry are deep, opposition is often formidable, and the responsibilities seem overwhelming. To serve as Christ's undershepherd, as one responsible for the proclamation of God's eternal truth, and to care for the souls of His people as one who will give an account, is a monumental task. While the joys of serving in the vineyard of Christ as His fellow-laborer are many and often exhilarating, there is no denying the fact that all ministers are in over their heads. In the fight against sin and the schemes of the Evil One, they are outnumbered, surrounded, and all too aware of their manifold weaknesses. So, when the waves of ministerial despair begin to roll over the pastor, where does he turn? All too often he turns inward and begins questioning

whether he really heard God's call correctly. Any pastor can describe those days when the thought of doing almost anything else besides praying, preaching, leading, and correcting is overwhelmingly inviting. It is at these times of desperate personal doubt that the knowledge that God has drafted him to be his spokesman, and fitted him for the task, can be the life-belt or life-ring he needs.

There is great benefit in being able to reflect on the fact that as a minister, you did not take this upon yourself; rather, God called you, and gifted you, and entrusted you with a specific and powerful message. Further, this call and these gifts were rigorously examined by the church, and through their prayerful and personal affirmation, you were commissioned to represent Christ as an undershepherd among the flock of God, charged with Christ's message, and granted the privilege of extending the grace of Christ to the world. As such, ordination becomes a strong platform of assurance in the time of storm, and firmly directs the pastor's heart and mind back to the Rock of his calling and his salvation, the Lord Christ, the Head of the church.

2) *Accountability*: Ordination, properly and rigorously done, impresses upon the man that he dare not get creative with the message entrusted to him. Neither can he lessen the diligence with which he governs his personal pursuit of holiness lest his character cease to measure up to the standards to which he has been called. Simply put, the ordained minister is the accountable minister. He is not free now to pursue his own kingdom or craft his own message, or live according to his own standards. He is a man under orders. He is a man who has acknowledged his accountability to the Lord and the church through the vows he has taken. Through the process of ordination he has been charged with a high duty, both to Christ and to his people.

The great benefit of this divine accountability is that it gives the pastor the great freedom to stand firm. Is the culture clamoring for a different message? Are people upset? Are the pressures of the day bringing strong temptations to compromise the message or the manner of biblical ministry? As an ordained minister you can say, 'Long before I met any of you I was given a direct charge by God to tell the truth, His truth. Given the choice whether to disappoint you or Him, I must abide with Him.'

Today, the pressure to fill auditoriums and services has driven many pastors to place the felt needs, or tastes, of the people above their duty to Christ. On every hand we hear of the gospel being molded into a non-confrontative message intended to meet felt needs and impress the sinful heart. And, by most standards, this new philosophy of church life is working, as more and more auditoriums are filled with people hungry for a message that will affirm that they are actually on fairly good terms with the Almighty. But the biblical message is the message of the cross. It cuts right across the grain of the modern age's preoccupation with pride, tearing down the facade and exposing the wretchedness of the human heart.

Unfortunately, while the modern 'un-gospel' may fill seats, it is the true gospel of sin and grace that is 'the power of God unto salvation' (Rom. 1:16). God has determined that it is through the message of the cross (1 Cor. 1:17) that He will save sinners, and has entrusted this message to men who through the 'foolishness of the message preached' (1 Cor. 1:21) will be His heralds of salvation. It ought to become more and more the case that men, having been directly called by God and charged by the church with the biblical message, resist the powerful temptations to compromise the truth of the gospel and stand firm for the message of the One who called them to be His representatives.

3) *Authority*: The last benefit of a serious ordination experience relates to the authority invested in the minister to carry out his tasks in a way that cannot be ignored in the world. I have long marveled at Paul's exhortation to Titus in Titus 2:15. After a full chapter of specific stipulations for Titus' ministry to the people of Crete, Paul interjects this incredible command: 'These things speak and exhort and reprove with all authority. Let no one disregard you.'

What the world needs today is men with a message so powerful that they can't be ignored. But just how was Titus to minister in Crete in a way that those who heard his message could not disregard him? The answer is that he was to serve in the very authority of Christ, granted to him as Christ's appointed spokesman. The ancient herald went forth with all the authority of his master invested in him. When he spoke, the people were to hear and obey as though the king himself was present. In a very real way this relates to the authority with which the minister of Christ performs his duties today in the church.

Knowing that he has been drafted, fitted for ministry, entrusted with a message, and sent out in the name of the Lord, the minister ought to demonstrate the proper authority in his every action. It is not a proud or arrogant authority, nor a tyranny, nor a selfish domination; all of these would be a singular affront to the One whose commission forms the basis of his ministry. Rather, it is an authority that is displayed in adoration of the Lord, humility before the Lord, boldness for the Lord, and absolute loyalty to the Lord and His truth. This authority is displayed at the same time in powerful exhortation and patient love. It is servant-leadership whose meekness and might are reminiscent of the Master Himself.

But just where is such authority impressed upon the heart of the man? It is the ordination process that presents just the right opportunity for the church and its leaders to drive this thought deeply into the heart of the man:

> *You are not your own; you are a man under orders. And the One who has drafted you and signed your orders expects that you will carry them out in a manner worthy of him, and in such a way that his authority and his kingdom cannot be ignored. Now go, labor, work, and do your duty well knowing that it is the greatest privilege under heaven to be in the personal service of the Almighty.*

Benefits for the Church

While the ordained minister benefits greatly from ordination done well, it is the church that reaps the greatest benefit. Through the rigors of ordination, the health of the church is both enhanced and protected. The growth of the body, being so dependent upon the teaching of the Word and the proper administration of pastoral duty, is promoted and assured when God's men are appointed to its pulpits. In addition, the health of the body is protected from tyranny and error as the pastoral office is judiciously guarded against any who would fill it apart from God's evident call. Ordination brings great benefit to the church in the areas of *provision* and *protection*.

1) *Provision for the Church*: In Ephesians 4:1-16 Paul describes the way in which Christ builds His church, provides for her health, and protects her from division. The unity of the body, already in existence in the Spirit, is to be preserved with all diligence (v. 3). The great threat to the unity of the body is the ever-present winds of error that swirl about the church and cause division (v. 14). In the center of this great text Paul explains God's divine

method for maintaining the unity and overall health of the church. Christ has given men, gifted and holy men, to the church in order that, through their teaching and leadership, the church will grow strong, maintain spiritual health and vitality, and succeed in the work of Christ in the world (vv. 11-13). That the health of the church is dependent in a large way upon the faithful ministry of these men is foundational to Paul's argument both here and everywhere he is concerned with the church (see also 1 Tim. 3:1-7; Titus 1:6-9; 2 Tim. 2:2, 24-26).

If the presence of divinely appointed men is essential to the health of the church, it is clear that it is in the church's best interest to maintain a high view of pastoral ministry, and the proclamation of the Word. Ordination, done well, provides a platform for the ongoing recognition that the preaching ministry is essential to the church's health. The higher the standards for ministry, and the expectations for ministry, the greater will be the church's honor and value of that ministry. And where the church honors and values the men and the message God has entrusted to them, the church will remain strong and vibrant in its unity and its testimony before a watching world.

2) *Protection for the Church*: The Scripture is full of warnings about the danger of allowing false teachers to occupy positions of influence in the church (see Ezek. 34; Mal. 3:1-5, 11; 2 Tim. 2:17; 4:1-5; 2 Pet. 2:1; Jude 1-4). And while the effects may not be as immediate or far-reaching, the consequences of allowing men into pastoral positions who are not called by God can be devastating to a church and its people. Countless churches struggle to recapture any vital ministry following the moral failure of a pastor. And in many such cases, upon close examination, it is found that the man's life had shown cracks in its foundation for years. Less sensational but equally

alarming is the vast number of churches whose struggle for survival is genuinely hampered because their pastor, despite a genuine heart for God, simply can't preach. Services are held, songs sung, and messages delivered, but there is no sense that the authority of God pervades the ministry of His Word, and the people begin to waste away due to biblical malnutrition.

While ordination as a process will not necessarily solve all the problems, it can help protect the church from those whose lives, or message, or gifts do not measure up to God's standards. Isn't it about time that we expected more from those who would stand before us as God's ministers? The church must reaffirm its dedication to having only God's men in leadership. When it does so, it focuses itself on the centrality of preaching and renews appreciation for the preaching office. It reaffirms the centrality of Christlikeness in its mission and message and demands that her ministers measure up.

Where the call of God is not conspicuously displayed in the man's character, desire, knowledge, and gifts, the church must not confer the right to minister. To do so is to settle for less than God's design, and risk at least the spiritual boredom of ministerial ineffectiveness, and at worst, the disastrous consequences of known and vital error.

3

The Man Whom God Appoints: Character and Desire

The most serious questions facing both the candidate and the church in the ordination process concern the measure of the man. Just what are we looking for? What are the distinguishing marks of a man's life that come as a result of God's call? And how do we measure them? These questions must be answered according to the truth of Scripture which, providentially, is clearly set out for us.

The Distinguishing Marks of God's Appointment

The entrance to public ministry has historically been divided into two stages. First, there is the internal call of God to the man by which God begins the process. Bannerman states:

> There is a distinction, and a most important one in the argument, to be drawn between the title to the *possession* of the ministerial office, and the title to the *exercise* of the ministerial office. The former, or the right to the office is the gift immediately of Christ; His call, directly addressed to the individual, gives him this first right. The latter, or the right to the exercise of the office, is also the gift of Christ; not however, immediately or directly bestowed, but conferred through the regular and outward appointment of the Church. The first, or a right to the ministerial office, is one involved in the call of the Savior Himself, addressed and announced to the individual by the bestowment upon him of those special gifts and graces of a spiritual kind which alone can qualify him for the office.[1] (Italics in the original.)

1   James Bannerman, *The Church of Christ* (reprint of 1869 ed., Banner of Truth, 1974) vol. 1:431.

It is the nature of this internal call, from Christ to the man, that occupies our attention here. What does it look like? How may it fairly be assessed to be of God? If, as stated above, God first drafts the man and then moves to fit him for ministry, what evidence will there be of this special work of God that can be used to demonstrate to both the man and the church that the call is of God?

This question reminds me of the medical field, and its ways of determining the presence of disease-causing agents in the body. Certain viruses are hard to detect directly. Yet their presence causes the body to produce anti-bodies which can be detected. The presence of one testifies to the reality of the other. And so it is in the call to ministry: *where the call of God is extended to the heart of a man, certain marks of that call appear as God moves to fit that man for pastoral ministry.* John Calvin put it well: 'Those whom the Lord has destined for such high office, he first supplies with the arms required to fulfill it, that they may not come empty-handed and unprepared.'[2]

The work of God in fitting a man to be his herald may be seen in four areas of the man's life: Character, Desire, Message, and Ministerial Gifts. As he calls a man, God begins molding his character and creating a proper desire for ministry. This work of God becomes more and more evident through the man's display of talents and ministerial gifts necessary to the performance of the ministry. That the man has been called of God is finally seen in that his message is consistent with the message entrusted to others historically and defined by the truth of Scripture.

The order in which these four areas are discussed does not imply that they are worked out in the man sequentially. The crafting of a man to be God's herald is

---

2   John Calvin, *Institutes of the Christian Religion*, ed. John T. McNeil; trans. by Ford Lewis Battles, Westminster Press, 2:1,063.

a mysterious process that proceeds differently in each. And yet, at the base of it all lies character. Even as God is at work shaping desire and growing a man in the areas of knowledge and ability, the first and most visible mark of the called man is godly character. While great gifts and broad knowledge are certainly a blessing in public ministry, no amount of academic or ministerial brilliance matters if the man is not first known to be conspicuously holy.

Character

The Scripture is clear that God's herald will represent the One who called him through the message of his life as well as his lips. In 1 Timothy 3:1-7 and Titus 1:5-9 Paul clearly declares that character matters. In fact, in view of the place given to character in selecting leaders, it is fair to say that it forms the foundation of a man's ministry. But, as with many Scriptural norms, this one is under fire today. Our society's rising tendency to overlook character in favor of ability has already begun infecting the church. To our shame we are forced to ask: *Does character matter in the church today, and especially in the lives of its leadership?*

Not long ago in my area of the country a prominent pastor fell into immoral living, to which he eventually confessed. After a stormy exit from his position of ministry, he resurfaced only three months later to assume preaching and teaching duties in another church. The reason? It seems that there was a belief on his part, and on the part of others he respected, that his gifts were so grand and his teaching so beneficial that to keep him from preaching would be a great disservice to the kingdom. Besides, he had repented and was forgiven, so why shouldn't he re-enter public ministry?

At issue is the relationship between ministry, character, and talent. It seems in our day that talent, and more to the point, spiritual productivity (e.g. getting the job done in a way that 'blesses' people, and brings them back) carries vastly more weight than the personal character of the man when it comes to affirming a man for pastoral ministry. But is talent more important to God than character? As we will see, God makes the man, and extends to him the gifts and graces necessary. To determine that a particular man is necessary to the Kingdom regardless of known character flaws, is to forget that God can raise up all the men He wants. He is not so in need of heralds that He can be forced by man's indiscretion to use those whose character is lacking. We must never forget that should He so desire, He can draft the rocks and cause them to cry out! Character matters, and it is a man's character that forms the foundation of his ministry because it gives credibility to his message. While great talent and ministerial ability are necessary, they are not sufficient. Where personal integrity and godly character are lacking, no amount of brilliance can compensate. As Robert Murray McCheyne so brilliantly put it: 'It is not great gifts that God blesses so much as it is great likeness to Christ.'

God demands that His heralds be men of godly character. It is telling that Paul, exhorting Timothy in the ways of leadership development, demands that he invest his time in 'faithful' men (2 Tim. 2:2). Proven character is everywhere seen as a prelude to position. The very first mark of God in the life is seen not in ability, but in holy living. To enter the service of Christ as a leader in the church without approved character is dangerous to the man and the church. It is also hypocritical to proclaim a message with your words that is not matched by your life.

Further, success in ministry is dependent upon godly character. So much of a man's usefulness in the lives of others is built on the testimony of his life. Paul himself called upon his followers to imitate him, but only as he was an imitator of Christ (1 Cor. 11:1). When a pastor teaches, he is trying to change the way people think and live. He is earnestly bringing the truth of God's Word to bear on every facet of life in order to see lives conformed to the image of Jesus. That is what he is doing officially. But unofficially he is saying this to all who hear him: *You need to accept what I am saying as God's truth and obey it; and if you do accept what I am telling you, and do it, your life will look like mine!* All Christians, but especially those charged with the authoritative proclamation of the Word, are living examples of what our listeners' lives will look like if they follow what we tell them to do. This means there is no room for secret habits of sin, hidden closets of wickedness, or even minor concessions in the areas of honesty and integrity. Simply put, character matters, and ordination is God's way both to critique a man's character, and to drive the expectations of God so deeply into the man that he never forgets the high calling he has received.

The first area of critique in the process of ordination must be this: *Does the man's life measure up? Is it distinctively holy and representative of what God demands?*

Historically, the first area of character examined in a man desiring to enter public ministry is his standing in grace. While today the fact of a man's regeneration by the Holy Spirit and the subsequent exhibition of true repentance and saving faith are largely taken as a given, it was not always so. Writing in the mid-seventeenth century, the great Puritan pastor Richard Baxter considered it a matter of first importance for preachers to strenuously examine the reality of their own salvation: 'And first, and above all, *see that the work of saving grace be thoroughly wrought on your own souls.*'[3] Baxter goes on

---

3   Richard Baxter, *The Reformed Pastor*, in Baxter's *Practical Works*, Soli Deo Gloria, 4:423 (italics in the original).

to stress the disastrous consequence to both the man and
the church when an unregenerate man is affirmed for
public ministry:

> Verily, it is the common danger and calamity of the
> church, to have unregenerate and inexperienced pastors;
> and to have so many men become preachers before they
> are Christians; to be sanctified by dedication to the altar
> as God's priests, before they are sanctified by hearty
> dedication to Christ as his disciples; and so to worship
> an unknown God, and to preach an unknown Christ,
> an unknown Spirit, an unknown state of holiness and
> communion with God, and a glory that is unknown, and
> like to be unknown to them for ever. He is like to be but
> a heartless preacher, that hath not the Christ and grace
> he preacheth in his heart.[4]

Centuries later, another pastor lays the same charge to
those who would stand as God's heralds. In *Words to
Winners of Souls*, Horatius Bonar stresses the necessity of
careful examination of a man's salvation as the beginning
point of ministry:

> The *true* minister must be a *true* Christian. He must
> be called by God before he can call others to God. The
> Apostle Paul thus states the matter: '*God...hath reconciled
> us to himself by Jesus Christ, and hath given to us the ministry
> of reconciliation*' (2 Corinthians 5:18). They were first
> reconciled, and then they had given to them the ministry
> of reconciliation. Are we *ministers* reconciled? It is but
> reasonable that a man who is to act as a spiritual guide
> to others should himself know the way of salvation.[5]

The man that God appoints as His spokesman will first
have been transformed by His grace. And yet, it must

---

4   Ibid, p. 423.
5   Horatius Bonar, *Words to Winners of Souls*, Hegg Bros, 1985, p. 13 (italics
     in the original).

not be taken for granted that all who volunteer to speak for God have experienced saving grace. As questions regarding the declining power and influence of the church in society grow, it is time to recognize that such would be the case if more and more pulpits were occupied by men who, regardless of ability and personality, are themselves strangers to grace. As Bonar summarizes it:

> The mere multiplying of men calling themselves ministers of Christ will avail little. They may be but 'cumberers of the ground'. They may be like Achan, troubling the camp.... Can the multiplication of such ministers, to whatever amount, be counted a blessing to a people?[6]

Surely the answer is a resounding 'No!' Those charged with affirming men to labor in the vineyard of the church as Christ's spokesmen must take great pains to see that the fingerprints of redeeming grace are to be found all over the man.

Following the question of true conversion, it is the daily character of a man's life that demands the focused attention of the ordination process. Much has been written, and rightly so, on the qualifications Paul sets down for spiritual leaders in 1 Timothy 3:1-7 and Titus 1:6-9. To these can be added Peter's remarks on leadership in 1 Peter 5:1-3.[7] For our purposes here it is necessary only to make some general observations about what the presence of these qualifications, and their nature, demand of the ordination process.

First, it is clear that the process of examining a man's life must take into consideration the full range of his character. The qualifications fall roughly into two categories:

---

6   Ibid, p. 7.

7   Several works have excellent discussions on the specific qualifications listed in these passages. See John MacArthur, Jr; *Rediscovering Pastoral Ministry*, Word, 1995, pp. 87ff; Bruce Stabbert, *The Team Concept*, Hegg Bros, p. 131ff.

personal and relational. The reality of Christ must be conspicuous both in the area of personal spirituality, and in his relationships with wife, family, fellow-believers, and the world.

Secondly, the nature of these qualifications demand that the critique of a man's life be done over time. For example, the health of a marriage, and the skill with which a man manages his household, cannot be determined in one home visit or a two-hour interview. To evaluate the spiritual maturity described by these qualifications demands that someone have a front row seat on the man's life, and have first hand knowledge over time of his life's testimony.

Thirdly, given that a man's character must be evaluated at the deepest levels, and over time, it is clear that the process of ordination demands the participation of the church family. Where ordination is reduced to a mere academic examination, the congregation is usually included only as an audience for the final commissioning. But where it is done well, the congregation becomes the essential starting place of affirmation. Where a local church body is well taught concerning God's processes of drafting and fitting men for ministry, they will be watchful for God's hand on the lives of men.

Lastly, it must be seen that there is a close and necessary connection between the qualifications demanded, and the ability to minister in Christ's place effectively. It is not just necessary to be gentle, uncontentious, and well-respected by unbelievers in order to enter the office of spiritual leadership. The full set of qualities of life and relationship are essential to ongoing, effective, God-blessed ministry. What God expects in a man at the starting line is what he demands of the man throughout the race. In fact, where the luster and purity of these qualities fade in the life of the minister, he is in grave danger of being pulled from the race and disqualified.

But before moving on from the subject of ministerial character, another important question must be raised. What does a life look like that measures up to the biblical standards? What kind of spiritual portrait do all of these several qualifications create? Fortunately, Paul helps answer these questions in 2 Timothy 1:6-14, in his great charge to Timothy. In what could provide a brilliant foundation for a commissioning service sermon, this text gives us Paul's inspired comments on the areas of pastoral character and practice. While this text does not explicitly touch on all the character qualities mentioned in 1 Timothy and Titus, it does give one example of what God expects from a man in whom these qualities are to be present and obvious.

Since we will be looking at several texts in 2 Timothy over the course of the book, it is helpful to provide just a brief understanding of where this lively epistle fits into the lives and ministries of Paul and his prodigy, Timothy. In this, the last of Paul's canonical letters, it is evident that his life is drawing to a close (4:6-8). He is anxious to leave Timothy fully prepared and motivated to carry on the ministry that has been entrusted to him (1:6). The letter is a very personal, yet serious and forceful, exhortation to Timothy to do the job God has drafted him to do. And as Paul reminds Timothy of some essentials of pastoral ministry, we get a grand reminder of three things that God expects of those He appoints.

1. An Evident and Sincere Faith

> 1:5: For I am mindful of the sincere faith within you, which first dwelt in your grandmother Lois, and your mother Eunice, and I am sure that it is in you as well.

Paul begins with a strong affirmation of Timothy as a child of God. As stated above, this remains the necessary starting point for ministry. That Paul continues to remind

Timothy of his salvation, even as Timothy is actively engaged in pastoral ministry, demonstrates the utter necessity of a vibrant and ever-present realization of personal regeneration in the life of the minister. Those to whom God has entrusted His message, and the care and feeding of souls, must never wander far from the miracle of personal salvation. The daily contemplation of your personal weakness, sin, and remaining depravity will bring your heart running back to the cross, and keep your pride at bay, despite the ministerial success you may enjoy. Where the fire of personal deliverance from sin and the warmth of eternal acceptance by the Almighty grows cold, so too will the heat of your ministry.

2. Confidence not Timidity in the Face of Ministerial Challenge

> 1:6, 7: And for this reason I remind you to kindle afresh the gift of God which is in you through the laying on of my hands. For God has not given us a spirit of timidity, but of power and love and discipline.

From the flow of Paul's exhortation it is clear that Timothy needed some not-so-gentle reminding that the ministry entrusted to him could never be accomplished if he gave in to the temptation of timidity. Based on the numerous times Paul has to exhort him to fight and be strong (1 Tim. 1:18-19; 4:12ff; 2 Tim. 1:7; 2:2-6; 3:14; 4:5), many commentators have suggested that Timothy was a weak person, often tempted to quit in the face of opposition, and not what one would call a strong leader. Even if this can not be dogmatically known, it is at least apparent from 2 Timothy 1:6, 7 that Timothy was in need of a strong charge in order to move him from the position of complacency he apparently was occupying.

Paul first reminds Timothy that the fire of ministry entrusted to him is in danger of going out, and needs to be 'rekindled'. Apparently Paul makes this assessment based on what he knows of Timothy's present ministerial posture. His strong exhortation that a 'spirit of timidity' is inconsistent with the God-given ministry of pastoring clearly suggests that Timothy, for whatever reasons, had retreated from a vibrant, robust posture in his ministry to the church. While gentleness is a must for the pastor, timidity is forbidden. What is needed from God's herald is a confidence that is recognizable as having come from God, and rests upon the call of God.

That this confidence is not based on human abilities or even the result of natural personality traits is seen in 2 Corinthians 2:14-4:7. Here, in an extended discussion on public ministry Paul shows, first, that the ministry of gospel proclamation is so grand that no man is, of himself, adequate to do it (2:14-16). And yet, secondly, those so engaged find that they have been made adequate by God Himself (3:4-6). Consequently, the man involved in gospel ministry is ever aware of his innate commonness and inadequacy, but is compelled to diligent and conspicuous ministry by the knowledge that the treasure he carries and has been charged to dispense, demands unceasing confidence, courage and complete dedication (4:7).

Paul describes what such a confidence looks like in 2 Timothy 1:7. What does God's herald look like when the various character qualities demanded of him are all rolled together, put into shoe leather, and pushed out on the public platform? Rather than being known for a 'spirit of timidity', those in whom the fire of God's call burns brightly will be seen to demonstrate 'power and love and discipline'.

Power: Paul has already shown that whatever ministerial gifts Timothy possesses, they arise not from his natural abilities but are God's gifts. His position, and the right to exercise it, has come as 'the gift of God' (v. 6). Further, the clear meaning of verse 7 is that, while the 'spirit of timidity' does not come from God, the 'power and love and discipline' do. Consequently, the power here described must be a spiritual power derived from the fact that the preacher represents the One who drafted him, and operates in and with His authority. In simple terms this means that the herald of God has been called to operate courageously, with a confidence grounded in the power and authority of God Himself.

Primarily, this power is attached to the Word that has been entrusted to the herald. Paul proclaims that the word of the gospel is the 'power of God unto salvation' (Rom. 1:16) and is the powerful weapon used by God's man to overcome error and opposition (2 Cor. 10:5-7). Even as Christ, the Living Word, is the 'power of God and the wisdom of God' (1 Cor. 1:24), so also the faithful proclamation of the Written Word, the word of the cross, is to those who are being saved 'the power of God' (1 Cor. 1:18). The man of God, entrusted with the Word of God, is 'adequate, fully equipped for every good work' (2 Tim. 3:17). Thus, where timidity characterizes a preacher, almost certainly it will be a result of the diminished role of Scripture in his life. But where the message entrusted is prized and faithfully proclaimed, the power of God will accompany the proclamation.

Love: when Paul attaches the demonstration of love to the demonstration of power in the life of Timothy, he certainly seems to be going against the flow of public opinion today. All too often we hear that a man is either a 'truth guy' or a 'love guy'. You can either be known for a powerful ministry, or a compassionate ministry, but usually not both! Having sat on numerous ordination councils, it never ceases to amaze me that so many buy into this view. Many men believe that their great intelligence and theological brilliance can make up for lacks in the areas of compassion, gentleness, and sensitivity to people, while others hope that their evident 'pastor's heart' can outweigh their lack of biblical and theological insight. Certainly Paul will have none of that! In his first letter to Timothy he exhorts the young minister to 'pay close attention to yourself and to your teaching' (1 Tim. 4:16). Depending on a man's natural tendency, he usually focuses on one or the other. But Paul is clear: *it is not either your life or your doctrine; it is both!* God does not send out men who are only half equipped for the task of representing Him. When He drafts a man, and equips him, He sends him out with both a spirit of power and a spirit of love.

It must be seen that, as with power, the spirit of love in the minister arises not so much out of natural personality, but is a gift of God. This love, then, will be a reflection of God's love, and will demonstrate itself not only in the man's sincere love for God and His truth, but also a deep compassion for people accompanied by a loving compulsion to seek after them, aid them, and extend the grace of Christ to them. How insightful is the comment often heard that 'one should not take the job of shepherd until he learns to love the smell of sheep!'

Discipline: the God-given posture of pastoral ministry includes power, and love, and discipline. Here Paul states that the herald of God will be a man of soberness and sound judgment. He will be prudent, self-controlled, and settled. While the timid man is apt to move from plan to plan, ever being blown around by the latest wind of doctrine or seminar formula, the herald of God has his mind tightly moored to the truth once and for all delivered by his Master. Simply put, the man God places into ministry is a man with a disciplined mind. He is, and must be, a good student, a thinker, capable of deep reflection, with the ability to discern truth from error and camp on it.

So, what does it look like when the character qualities demanded of ministers come together in real life situations? While Paul's charge to Timothy does not give an exhaustive description, this at least is clear: *The man God calls and places into ministry will be courageous in knowing and proclaiming the Word, conspicuous in knowing and loving people, and a diligent thinker and sound decision-maker.*

3. Courage, not Compromise, in Defence of the Gospel

> 1:8: Therefore, do not be ashamed of the testimony of our Lord, or of me, his prisoner; but join me in suffering for the gospel according to the power of God.

Because God expects his heralds to display power, love, and discipline in their ministry, it is the height of inconsistency for them to be ashamed of any part of the message He has entrusted to them. Is Paul suggesting that he has received news regarding Timothy that leads him to believe that his disciple is backing away from some of the truth? Perhaps. And if so, Timothy is only guilty of falling to the temptation that hounds every preacher of the gospel. How often are we tempted to downplay or soften parts of biblical truth in an attempt to stay dry on the ocean of ministry? With all the other challenges of pastoral practice, who needs the waves of controversy flooding into the boat? But when we read Paul's exhortation to Timothy, it is clear that any tendency to shy away from the truth and its faithful proclamation is unacceptable.

When Paul commands Timothy against being 'ashamed of the testimony of our Lord' and exhorts him to join in 'suffering for the gospel', two things jump out at us. First, the fact that Timothy could be ashamed of the truth's testimony means that *some parts of the message God entrusts to us will be offensive to the audience He commands us to address.* If the message carried no offence to the audience, there would be no temptation to be ashamed of it. Secondly, it is clearly Paul's point that *when the herald adheres faithfully and unashamedly to the message, he may well be called upon to suffer for the message.*

But what does this have to do with character? Is this not better suited to the area of doctrinal examination? Yes, and no. While the content of the message is certainly to be examined, any willingness to edit or compromise or trivialize the message of God is really a question of character. Has the man the stuff to stand by the message? Has he the courage and strength of character to remain faithful to the orders received? Simply put, can he be trusted to walk in the truth, to tell the truth, and, if need be, to suffer for the truth? While the individual character qualities given by Paul to Timothy and Titus are certainly a necessary plumb line, the examination of every candidate for ordination must extend beyond this list to the composite picture of the man as demonstrated in his evidence of genuine faith, his ministerial confidence, and his doctrinal courage.

Desire

In 1 Timothy 3:1 Paul explains that the man who 'aspires to the office of overseer' manifests a laudable desire. Since the work of pastoral oversight is said to be 'a fine work' the desire for that work must also be seen as a good and righteous desire. When we consider Paul's message to the Ephesian elders in Acts 20:28 that it is 'the Holy Spirit (who) has made you overseers, to shepherd the church of God which he purchased with his own blood', it is clear that the placing of men into ministry is a work initiated by God. In drafting and appointing a man to ministry, God acts to place a righteous desire for ministry upon the man's heart.

Unfortunately, it is all too often assumed that any man claiming this desire for ministry must be called of God. And yet it must be agreed that if the desire for ministry is truly from God, then that desire for ministry will be the right kind of desire. That is, it will mirror the attitudes and motives of the Great Shepherd of God's sheep, Jesus Christ Himself. This will demonstrate itself in the proper ministerial attitude: an attitude that prefers the way of the cross to the applause of the crowd, that defines success as faithfulness, that finds joy in suffering, that protects and proclaims the truth despite cultural pressures, and that refuses to do God's work man's way, regardless of how the world around may clamor for the glamorous.

The proper attitude of ministry is actually the flower of godly character. *How* a man operates among Christ's sheep must, of necessity, be a reflection of *who* he is as Christ's under-shepherd. The right attitude of ministry is built on possessing the correct character of life.

When Paul, in 1 Timothy 3:1, states that there is a desire within the man seeking pastoral ministry, he brings up the question as to the make-up of that desire. Just what is the nature and object of this desire? Here we enter into a discussion of a man's *motive* for entering ministry. As has been shown, when God drafts a man for the preaching ministry, He also crafts in that man the necessary character. But beyond that, He also impresses upon that man the proper attitude of ministry. Just as a man's character is a validation of God's call on his life, so also the proper attitude toward the job of pastoring is a display that the desire in his heart is of God.

The area of ministerial attitude is much obscured to-day. Increasingly, pastors are being told to act more as C.E.O.'s than shepherds. Seminars tout the latest formulas for growing churches, managing resources, maximizing competitive advantage, and exploiting the 'niche' in the market that best fits with your church's strengths. It is abundantly clear that, for many congregations and pastors today, 'success' is defined by numerical growth, high visibility in the community, a sense of professionalism, and being recognized as able to compete with all that the unbelieving world offers to the entertainment consumer. Bigger is better. Excitement and glamour, combined with relevance and convenience, add up to powerful ministries bursting with the blessing of God. This attitude to ministry sincerely believes that God is most glorified when the church is recognized by the community as exciting, successful, powerful, glamorous, inviting, accepting, and, above all, culturally relevant.

Unfortunately, the appeal of the grand and glorious has captured the attention of far too many congregations, and their leaderships. The lure of popularity and public acclaim has dramatically altered the definition of ministerial success away from its pure biblical form. Simply put, the mark of a herald's success is not what the audience thinks of him; it is what the king thinks of him. The basic definition of ministerial success is, and has always been, faithfulness. Is the man faithful to God? Is he faithful to the message entrusted to him? Is he faithful to proclaim the message in all power and love and discipline, as he has been instructed? It is just at this point that the popular, contemporary attitude of ministry – what Luther would have called a ministry of glory – collides and conflicts with the proper attitude stressed in God's Word. This attitude is best described as a ministry of the cross. When God drafts a herald, He instructs him to walk in the way of the cross. It is a man's understanding of the way of the cross, with its twin privileges of suffering and joy, that will display the reality of God's call on his life. The ordination process, correctly understood and practised, will not only examine the character of a man's life, but will also assess the attitude of his heart toward the ministry to see if it is ever in the shadow of Calvary's cross.

As noted above, Paul's instructions to Timothy in 2 Timothy 1:6-14 are very instructive concerning the

particulars of gospel ministry. Conspicuous among them
is the call to 'join in suffering for the gospel according
to the power of God' (v. 8). This theme of willing and
voluntary suffering for the truth is a cornerstone of the
way of the cross. In verse 11 Paul states that he was
appointed a herald of the gospel message, and 'for this
reason, I also suffer these things' (v. 12). That suffering is
connected with proclaiming the truth is to Paul a given
for the gospel preacher. In Colossians 1:24 Paul adds
a second component of this 'ministry of the cross': 'Now
I rejoice in my sufferings for your sake...' Far from being
discouraged by the opposition and suffering which
confronted him in his ministry of God's Word, Paul
finds great joy in knowing that he is effecting God's
work in the world. Once again the point must be made
that ministerial success is always defined by the herald
as *faithfulness to the King, His message, and His work.*

J. A. O. Preus, in a brilliant article on the proper mindset
for gospel ministry, demonstrates that the pattern for
faithful church leadership is the Savior himself.[8] He says:
'The pattern that Christ has established for his ministers
is his own path of suffering and joy.'[9] He goes on to say:

> As ministers of the cross, our ministry is a reflection of
> the ministry of Christ. In our call, Christ invites us to
> participate with him in his ministry of reconciliation. Our
> participation in Christ's ministry involves many things,
> among them the paradox of joyful suffering. In the light
> of Christ and on behalf of his body, the Church, we are
> granted a new way of suffering and of rejoicing, *which
> in many ways transforms our actions and our attitudes in the
> ministry.*[10]

---

8   J. A. O. Preus, 'Suffering and Joy: The Ministry as Participation in
    Christ's Cross', *Modern Reformation*, July/August, 1997, pp. 20-23.

9   Ibid, p. 20.

10 Ibid, p. 23; emphasis added.

Preus has hit the target dead center. When Christ came to earth, He did not come to do His own will, but the will of the Father. As His undershepherds, we are not free to do our own thing in order to find success in the religious marketplace of today's society. Rather we are to reflect Christ in all that we say and do. And the Christ of Scripture is the humble, suffering servant who, in spite of great opposition, false accusations, and public ridicule, remained faithful to the heavenly calling.

Today's pastors, and those men entering pastoral ministry, will be distinguished as authentic heralds of God by their willingness to live out Christ's attitude of ministry. I call this attitude the way of the cross. At its core lies an overriding preference to extend the truth of God to the world in such a way that God gets all the glory. Further, it is a radical conviction that God's power is perfected in weakness, and that it is not the stature of man but the sovereignty of God that accomplishes His spiritual ends. Lastly, it is a settled refusal not to substitute the acclaim of man for the approval of God, knowing that God is only using you to make disciples of Christ, not fans of the church. This attitude is a daily living out of the cross whereby the temptations to personal pride, independence, and the lust for applause are crucified. Anyone who thinks that building Christ's church is dependent upon their creativity in programming, their marketing savvy, or their ability to adapt the truth to fit the palate of the modern audience simply has not come to grips with what Scripture demands of the herald. Two passages considered briefly give us the simple picture of the attitude Christ brings to those He empowers to speak for Him.

In John 3:22-36 an incident is described where the disciples of John the Baptist come to him with some questions regarding Jesus. It seems that Jesus has begun cutting

into the crowd that usually followed John (v. 26). What
is interesting is that this pleases John greatly, for such
is the measure of success for the herald. John begins by
reminding his followers that he is not Christ (a welcome
reminder for pastors as well!) (v. 28). John is adamant
that he exists to point people to Christ, not to gain a following for himself. He is the friend, not the bridegroom,
and it is his greatest joy to see Jesus increase in fame and
influence, even though this means that he must decrease
in those things (vv. 29, 30). What a wonderful core prin-
ciple for today's pastor! The attitude of the cross brings
a man to a joyful downplaying of himself in order that
Christ might be magnified. There is no self-promotion
on the part of the faithful herald. He is not seeking the
spotlight, nor addicted to the applause of the crowd. He
is content to go further and further into the shadows as
the light of truth is focused more and more on the sweet-
ness of the Savior. And should the stray eye move back
to focus on him, his first task is, in reflecting the grace
and love of Christ, to re-direct that eye to Jesus.

Paul gives us another example of the proper ministerial
attitude in 2 Corinthians 4:1-10. After describing the
message and method of his ministry (vv. 1-6), he settles
in on a vivid portrayal of his self-perception as a minister
of God. The picture he paints in verses 7-10 is most vivid:

> But we have this treasure in earthen vessels, that the
> surpassing greatness of the power may be of God and
> not from ourselves; we are afflicted in every way, but not
> crushed; perplexed, but not despairing; persecuted, but
> not forsaken; struck down, but not destroyed; always
> carrying about in the body the dying of Jesus, that the
> life of Jesus also may be manifested in our body.

The treasure of the gospel message has been placed in
'earthen vessels'. What a picture! God has entrusted His
message to those who are best described as old clay pots.

In Paul's day, the clay pot was the most common dish of the household. It was not special, had no great value, was easily chipped, but just as easily replaced. Nothing about a clay pot captured anyone's attention. They existed in great numbers, and no one pot held any special value. How humbling for Paul to choose the clay pot to symbolize the minister of the gospel! His clear conclusion is that it is not the man alone that matters; no one man is indispensable. God can use anyone He chooses. Ministerial usefulness is a gift bestowed by God and we must never forget that. If we do, we will begin to think that we are a golden dish, special and worthy of the honor that belongs to Christ alone.

But Paul does not stop with a description of the pot. He goes on to show that the thing that makes the pot so very valuable is what it carries. When the message of the gospel is poured into the pot, it changes everything. Suddenly the pot has great value, great worth, great opportunity. Nothing has changed the pot; its new-found prestige has everything to do with the powerful truth it carries. And even though this message will subject the pot to all manner of opposition and suffering (vv. 8, 9) it is the joy of the minister to manifest the life of Christ to the world, even though it may often be the case that the minister has to identify really and personally with the dying of Christ (v. 10). The way of Christ is the way of the cross. And yet, the way of the cross, with all of its suffering, is paved with great joy, the pastor knowing that the life and love of Jesus are manifested through the faithfulness of his herald.

Summary

As we have seen, the man whom God appoints to be a pastoral leader in Christ's church will display the character God requires. Such a man will have courage and conviction. He will be capable of standing and delivering the message without compromise. And yet this strength of character and conviction does not translate into an attitude of pride and self-sufficiency. Rather, like Christ his Master, he realizes that it is the message, not the man, that matters in the long run. Further, he is dedicated to the glory of his Master, and not his own. He understands that the great strength of the King and the King's message is best displayed against the background of his own weakness. He refuses to take the credit or play to the applause of men. In short, he lives in the shadow of the cross which daily reforms his life, informs his message, and transforms his attitudes. He has come joyfully to echo the great cry of the apostle in Galatians 6:14: 'But may it never be that I should boast, except in the cross of our Lord Jesus Christ, through which the world has been crucified to me, and I to the world.'

4

The Man Whom God Appoints: Message and Gifts

The internal call of God to pastoral ministry is displayed initially in what a man *is*. His godly character and righteous desire for ministry are essential marks of God's appointment. But just as important is the weighing of what the man can *do*. Ministry is, at its core, service for God to people. It is an active, demanding, and all-consuming set of complex duties designed by God to accomplish his will in the lives of those it touches. In the process of ordination, it is essential not only to affirm who the man is in Christ (character and desire), but also what he has been divinely crafted to do for Christ. This demands a careful examination of the message the man carries, and the gifts with which he wields it.

The Message

Like the old saying goes, *the proof of the pudding is in the eating.* As a man who loves pudding, I understand what is meant here. Looks have some value when it comes to judging pudding. But, brother, it's the taste that matters! The same applies to identifying a man upon whom God has placed his hand in divine appointment to preach. If he has been truly called of God, the message he proclaims will be the truth as Scripture states it. The proof of the man is in the message.

Of all the components of the call to ministry, this is the one that is easiest to define and critique because it can be judged against objective standards. And yet it is increasingly the case that men are entering pastoral ministry with less than adequate knowledge of the Bible, theology, and pastoral ministry. As is sadly the case with character and ministerial attitude, all too often churches also settle for second best when they put men into pastoral positions who lack deep biblical knowledge and broad theological understanding. It is the place of the ordination process to consider a man's understanding of the message he claims to have been given by God to see if it squares with the message set down in Scripture. God's heralds will certainly be men who are under orders to proclaim the truth, the whole truth, and nothing but the truth. When the content of a man's message is at odds with the Scripture, it is clear evidence that, despite his worthiness in other areas, whatever desire he has for public ministry is not from God.

But there are great challenges presented to the church when called upon to pass judgment on a man's biblical knowledge, theological reflection, and doctrinal con-viction. The greatest is knowing that standard against which the man will be measured. A simple illustration will help.

Several years ago, as a young married man, I decided to seal off a backyard carport from the alley by installing a roll-down garage door. Since my dad was the ultimate handyman, I asked both his advice and assistance in getting the job done right. When the day arrived to do the work, Dad called to say he would be delayed. 'How hard can it be?' I asked myself, and started to frame in the opening for the door without him. After a couple hours of sawing and pounding, I stood proudly in front of the finished frame. When Dad arrived, he appeared with a strange angled metal tool and asked, 'Is it square?' In a matter of moments my work, as proud as I was of it, and as good as it appeared to me, was completely discredited by the metal square in the hands of my craftsman father. The work of my hands failed to stand the test when measured by the agreed-upon standard.

When a man is examined by the church through the ordination council, his work is being judged as well. Is it square? Is it orthodox? Does it align with the accepted standard? Yet my experience on ordination councils suggests that it is at this point that there exists great opportunity for both confusion and frustration for all those involved. For any ordination process to be successful and consistent it must have, as a tool of measurement, a defined, understood, and agreed upon 'truth template' that fairly represents the group conferring ordination. Those denominations and churches who adhere to an historic creed or confession have the best foundation for critique; those who do not, or who have crafted some doctrinal statement of their own, must go further to ensure that those doing the examination understand the standards, and do not change them or go beyond the boundaries set. Clearly, this area of standards is one where diligent work on the part of an ordaining body will be greatly rewarded with consistency and effectiveness in the ordination process.

In examining a man's understanding of biblical truth, Paul's words to Timothy and Titus give us biblical grounds for critique, and suggest some very useful categories for doing so. In referring to an overseer, Paul writes that those who occupy this office must 'hold fast the faithful word which is in accordance with the teaching, that he may be able both to exhort in sound doctrine, and to refute those who contradict' (Titus 1:9). Along the same lines Paul writes to Timothy that 'the Lord's bondservant must...[be] able to teach...with gentleness correcting those who are in opposition...' (2 Tim. 2:24, 25). God's herald must know the truth, must understand the relationship of the truth to the error that thrives in the world, and he must have the firm convictions for the truth necessary to proclaim and defend it. For practical purposes, the examination of a man's message may be broken down into three components: *knowledge, reflection,* and *conviction.*

1) Knowledge

To 'hold fast' the faithful word first demands a knowledge of it. This component of the man's message demands a comprehensive knowledge of the Bible, including both content and history. Does the candidate display a working use of Scripture and a broad familiarity with the facts it contains, the stories it tells, and the truths it teaches? Is he able to answer questions using Scripture and arguing from Scripture? Does he evidence a clear understanding of the flow of redemptive history and the roles played by various biblical books and authors?

This area of knowledge is like the building materials necessary to complete a construction project. Does the builder understand the various materials he needs to do a job? Can he locate them, gather them together, and understand how they fit together? The next component – *reflection* – looks at whether the builder can put the materials together in a thoughtful way and construct a meaningful and fair product.

2) Reflection

Knowing the truth is a necessary prerequisite to using the truth. Yet in between understanding and use is *reflection.* This component I define as the work necessary to form a consistent theological framework, showing serious thought in synthesizing the facts of Scripture into a coherent system. Does the candidate demonstrate that he has thought through biblical, theological, and practical issues enough to both understand their complexity, and to present his views fairly and persuasively? Too often men sitting for examination offer clichés and seminary definitions as answers to the council's questions. But Paul's exhortation to 'hold fast the word' is seen as a prerequisite to 'exhort[ing] in sound doctrine'. Such exhortation demands that the teacher has thought through the issues; that he has taken the facts of Scripture, viewed them through the lens of church history, and become personally invested in thoughtful reflection on the issues, their problems, and legitimate solutions. Few things are more distressing to an ordination council than a candidate who demonstrates no passion for personal theological wrestling and, instead, is content to give memorized answers to expected questions.

3) Conviction

As the first component relates to *foundational biblical knowledge,* and the second to *systematic theological reflection,* so the third component relates to *dogmatic and persuasive conviction.* A good definition of this dogmatic conviction is found in Paul's words to Timothy: 'You, however, continue in the things you have learned and become convinced of, knowing from whom you have learned them' (2 Tim. 3:14). Conviction is that resolute and continued stand for the truth of which the person has become convinced. It demands that the candidate take a stand, defend it, and hold to it in the face of objections and ridicule. But the great question is this: on what issues must the candidate demonstrate unbending dogmatism? It is at this point that the standards for ordination, set by the ordaining body, are absolutely necessary. They must draw the circle clearly to encompass all those areas in which dogmatic and persuasive conviction is essential, and to identify all other areas as those in which dogmatism is not necessary.

Ministerial Gifts

When God appoints a man He also builds into him the ministerial gifts necessary to a successful completion of the task assigned. Consequently, where God truly calls, there will be the growing expression of those gifts necessary to pastoral leadership. While character matters, and godly desire is essential, they are not enough. History is full of examples of pious young men who enter the ministry without the ability to teach, to preach, to lead, to care for people, and stand for the truth. But what they had in sincerity could never make up what they lacked in ability. C. H. Spurgeon spoke insightfully on this:

> How may a young man know whether he is called or not? That is a weighty enquiry, and I desire to treat it most solemnly. O for divine guidance in so doing! That hundreds have missed their way, and stumbled against a pulpit is sorrowfully evident from the fruitless ministries and decaying churches which surround us. It is a fearful calamity to a man to miss his calling, and to the church upon whom he imposes himself, his mistake involves an affliction of the most grievous kind.[1]

It has become almost commonplace in our day to make excuses for the poor ministerial performances of pastors. All too often we settle for pathetic preaching by lazy pastors, or poor leadership by clumsy pastors, or some other mediocre pastoral activity just because the man behind the pulpit is kind and gentle, and seems to have a good heart. Yet none of us would volunteer to have a kind and gracious doctor with poor surgical skills perform an emergency heart bypass on us! Why do we consider that the work of the ministry should be held to low standards? Why do we put up with preaching and leading that is, at best, exceedingly average? The answer is that we have forgotten that whom God calls and appoints, He also fully fits with the ministerial gifts to do the job, and do it well. When men, regardless of their personal

---

1   C.H. Spurgeon, David Otis Fuller, editor; *Spurgeon's Lectures to His Students*; Zondervan; Grand Rapids, 1945; p. 28.

piety and character, enter pastoral ministry without the ministerial gifts to do the job well, the church suffers greatly, and the men often crumble under the weight of failure. But this doesn't have to happen. Where ordination is correctly understood and practised, men who are not ready will be turned away. Only those men whose abilities in feeding and leading the flock give clear evidence of having been crafted and matured by God will be affirmed for public ministry. This is clearly better for the church, and ultimately for the men as well.

In examining a man's pastoral gifts it is helpful to divide them into two broad classes: those gifts necessary to *feed* the flock, and those used to *lead* it.

Feeding the Flock
Paul, in writing to both Timothy and Titus, stressed that those selected to serve as leaders in the church had to be 'able to teach' (1 Tim. 3:2; 2 Tim. 2:24), able to 'exhort' and 'refute' (Titus 1:9), and ready to 'correct' those who opposed the truth (2 Tim. 2:25). They were to teach the truth and repel error, and do both effectively. Candidates for ordination today must be held to the same standard.

What is at issue here is the ability of the candidate to communicate the truth of God. Remember, the herald was first and foremost a trusted individual who could be counted on to deliver the message given to him. Communication of the message was at the core of his job description. And yet, the task of evaluating the teaching ability of a man is no easy task. Today the task of pastoral communication takes many forms. Pastors are called upon to deliver the truth in private counsel and conversation as well as from the pulpit. In addition to verbal communication, the printed page is increasingly used as a vehicle for spreading God's truth. When you add to this the fact that different settings and audiences often demand differing abilities in communicating, the job of determining if a man has been gifted by God to speak his truth becomes dangerously subjective. But the challenge of such evaluation can be lessened to the degree that the ordaining body gives due consideration to the particular pastoral task assigned to the candidate, and the cultural setting in which it is to be carried out.

Take as an example a man desiring to be ordained as a pastor to children. His style of communication would be significantly different from that of a man intending to carry on a pulpit ministry as the primary teacher in a corporate worship setting. However, it must be understood that the difference must not be one of effectiveness, but rather of style. Both men must demonstrate divine giftedness in their own sphere of ministry even though each area will demand skills and sensitivities specific to it. Additionally, the cultural setting in which a man will minister must be taken into consideration. A man who ministers in a college town and interacts often with university students may require a more sharpened ability to present reasoned, logical arguments and understand philosophical points of view, while a man ministering in a small rural community may find great benefit in a more 'home spun' common sense orientation. Again, what is at issue is the effectiveness of the man in bringing the truth of God to bear on the lives of those to whom he is being sent.

In evaluating a man's ability to teach it is necessary to inject some objectivity into a largely subjective task. The communication of God's truth by a man appointed and duly gifted by God will at least be recognizable as being: (1) clear and understandable; (2) winsome and arresting; and (3) life-changing.

To be clear and understandable a message must make good use of language. It must not be confusing, but flow logically, giving the explanations the audience needs, and answering the questions they are asking. The message must not be hidden or obscured by the teacher's vocabulary, grammar, or organization; rather, the light of truth must be seen to shine brightly and clearly so that those listening see it, and recognize it as the truth. As has often been said, the best way to evaluate if someone is a teacher is to let them teach and then see if anyone learned anything! If you want to know if the message was clear and understandable, ask the audience – they'll know.

Good communicators, at all levels and in all areas, demonstrate a winsome and arresting character in their communication. They invite the ear to listen attentively, and hold their audience's attention sufficiently to bring them down the path from problem to solution, from confusion to clarity, from the mysterious to the known and understood. While much about good communication can be learned and improved over time, gifted teachers all begin with some ability to hold the attention of their audience.

Lastly, a man who has been appointed by God will be recognized by the spiritual effects the message has on the hearts of the hearers. Over time it will be recognized by his audience that the message he delivers comes in the power of God, is spiritually persuasive, and moves their hearts to act in obedience to the truth. Such a message, coming in God's authority, cannot be disregarded (Titus 2:15), is reasonable and persuasive to the heart (Acts 17:2-4), and impacts the heart in such a way that it is known to be of God (Luke 24:32).

The character and components of divinely anointed teaching cannot be examined except over time, and in conjunction with those who are being taught. For this reason, men seeking ordination must be given opportunities to teach, and to do so over a period of time to the same audience. Audio and video cassettes of a teaching series, along with personal attendance at teaching sessions, can give the ordaining council some indication of the man's ability. But it is vital as well to include the responses of those who, having sat under the man's teaching, can give valuable insights through personal interviews or well-designed surveys.

Leading the Flock

In 1 Timothy 3:4,5 Paul exhorts Timothy to appoint as an overseer only that man who 'manages his household well', for such management and leadership ability is essential if the man is to 'take care of the church of God'. That God-appointed men are to lead the church is further stated by Peter when he exhorts his fellow elders to 'shepherd the flock of God among you, exercising oversight' (1 Pet. 5:2). While the specific tasks involved are not mentioned, the manner of such leadership is clearly defined by Peter when he demands that they not act 'as lording it over those allotted to your charge, but proving to be examples to the flock' (1 Pet. 5:3). The demand to be exemplary extends not only to the man's character and the content of his message; it also defines the standard for his leadership activity in regard to his people management skills and style.

In assessing a man's leadership skills the church must follow the instruction of Paul and begin their examination in the candidate's home. As previously cited, Paul connects the management of the household (1 Tim. 3:4,5) and the proper control of children (Titus 1:6) with the tasks involved in caring for the church of God. Due consideration of the following four areas of leadership in the home and church will determine if the man's life demonstrates that he has been gifted by God to lead the church. In every case, critique of the man must begin with an examination of those lives entrusted to his leadership. Is a man a gifted leader? Look at the lives of those he leads.

1. Communicating Standards and Direction

In the home, and in the church, leadership begins with the setting of biblical standards for conduct, and the communication of direction to the group. Paul exhorted Titus to 'speak and exhort and reprove with all authority. Let no one disregard you' (Titus 2:15). Further, he was to 'speak confidently, so that those who have believed in God may be careful to engage in good deeds' (Titus 3:8). Leaders are to determine the biblical standards for everyday living, placing them clearly before those they are leading as authoritative and binding on them. They must do this both patiently and persuasively, for the best communication comes from the platform of compassion and care, and moves the listeners to trust and obedience. The great benefit of such leadership is seen when their followers walk in the paths of truth and display the fruit of righteousness in good deeds. Such leadership demands that first the man knows what God expects, then that he demonstrates it in his own life, and finally, that he communicates it clearly to those under his authority. This was ably demonstrated in the life of Ezra, one of the greatest leaders of the Old Testament. In undertaking the daunting task of re-establishing the religious activity of Israel in the re-built temple, he proved to be a leader sent from God. In Ezra 7:6 and 9 we are told that his efforts met with success 'because the hand of the LORD his God was upon him'. But in verse 10 we are given the reason for God's blessing: 'For Ezra had set his heart to study the law of the LORD, and to practice it, and to teach his statutes and ordinances in Israel.' No man should assume that he has been drafted by God to lead the church if he has not demonstrated in his personal and home life that he understands, obeys, and can clearly declare biblical standards for living.

2. Decision Making

In Philippians 1:9-11 Paul relates that his prayer for his beloved readers pertains to their great need of discernment. He prays 'that your love may abound still more and more in real knowledge and discernment, so that you may approve the things that are excellent...' While this is necessary for all believers, it is essential for godly leaders. Those who would lead the church must have a demonstrated ability to discern the best from the variety of options presented in the various situations of life. Such discernment is not based on emotion or whim but is the fruit of 'real knowledge'. It is the demonstration of true wisdom gained from laboring in the Word and prayer over time until the choices confronting the man are viewed clearly through the lens of Scripture.

In evaluating a man's discernment, his personal and home life are the place to start. First it must be asked: *is the man a decision maker*? Does he take appropriate action when decision time comes or is he prone to inaction? Does he show courage in making the tough decision or is he more apt to postpone the decision or pass the responsibility to someone else in the hope that the situation will work itself out? Paul, in trying to shake Timothy out of his ministerial slumber, forcefully reminded him that 'God has not given us a spirit of timidity, but of power and love and a sound mind' (2 Tim. 1:7). All leadership demands that decisions be made and that the leader not become paralyzed when action is needed.

Secondly, it is necessary to determine if the man makes decisions wisely. Those whom God places in leadership will not only be men of action; they will as well be men of righteousness and wisdom in determining the right action to take. Godly leaders approach each decision point prayerfully, understanding the value of patience, knowing the necessity of seeing and examining the options and situations as they really are, and insisting that all relevant biblical material be considered. Further, they prize the wisdom of others, and actively seek out the insights of wise counselors. They are known to their friends for the discipline and sound judgment displayed in the various decisions of their lives. They manage their affairs well, and it shows.

3. Stewardship

An essential leadership skill is the management of resources. Those who would lead and care for the church will have demonstrated over time that they can be trusted with time, people, money, and the other 'raw materials' necessary for any organization's success. It is interesting that Paul's most famous statement on the love of money is written to a man in a church leadership position. In 1 Timothy 6:3-19 Paul decries the arrogance of those who consider ministry a means of monetary gain (vv. 3-5), while he exhorts Timothy to remember that a correct view of money is essential to profitable service as a leader in the church (vv. 8-10). Jesus himself told us that if we look at a man's use of money, we will find out just where his heart's desires lie (see Matt. 6:19-21). It is essential that the lives of men desiring ordination be carefully examined to see if there is evidence of godly stewardship. Are their finances well-managed? Do they invest their time wisely? Are their lives free from habits or hobbies that consume their finances and time inordinately? Are they generous with their time, their talents and their money? Knowing how they have managed their home, would you trust them with the resources, both human and material, of the church? As is true with every other area of ministerial qualification, the men whom God appoints must be exemplary in the area of stewardship.

4. Conflict Resolution

The true character of a leader ought to shine the brightest when he is asked to deal with conflict and opposition. Here God's man must walk in a manner worthy of the gospel. Those pursuing ordination, as well as those

charged with their examination, must recognize that the
way God would have us deal with conflict and the way
we naturally react are vastly different. In evaluating
a man's leadership gifts in the area of conflict resolution,
two simple questions must be asked. First, does the man
deal with conflict? Does he recognize the destructive
nature of interpersonal conflict between people? Does he
understand the corrupting power of sin and error when
allowed to run rampant in the home and the church?
Does he move circumspectly, using biblical guidelines, to
uncover the root problem and then act tirelessly to bring
repentance, reconciliation and peace, even admitting his
own guilt when necessary? Or is he put off by conflict
and prone to ignore it, especially if it means confronting
another person or admitting personal wrongdoing?
In Galatians 6:1 Paul commands the 'spiritual' ones to
move courageously in dealing with situations where sin
has taken root. For, as Hebrews 12:15 reminds us, left
undealt with, spiritual problems are like bitter roots which
grow in the heart and, springing up, infect and defile all
those around them. To allow hard feelings and fractured
relationships to go unattended is to leave the hearts of
those involved ploughed and prepared for the seeds of
bitterness and division.

Secondly, does the man deal with conflict righteously? Paul deals with this question directly in the
New Testament. Spiritual men will approach conflict
situations 'in a spirit of gentleness' (Gal. 6:1) and when
correction is called for, it will be administered 'in gentleness' (2 Tim. 2:25). Further, when they are the re-
cipients of opposition or hurtful actions, they will bear
it with patience, even when they are unjustly accused
(2 Tim. 2:24). No believer is ever to respond to evil with
evil (Rom. 12:17), but rather is to overwhelm evil with
righteousness (Rom. 12:21). Such must especially be the
case among those appointed by God to be his represent-

atives in leading the church. As the refiner's fire is used to bring out the purity of the metal, so also conflict must bring out the godly character and leadership ability of the pastor. Where a man has demonstrated the courage to deal with conflict, and the ability to do so with gentleness, wisdom, and righteousness in his home, there is reason to believe that he has been drafted by God to serve as his undershepherd in the church.

Summary
In the last two chapters I have overviewed the four areas of a man's life that must be carefully examined through the process of ordination. If due consideration is given to all four areas (character, desire, message, and gift) it could well take years. And yet, most ordination processes revolve around a day or two of mostly academic examination. But if the preaching of the Word by men appointed and equipped by God is essential to the life of the church and the growth of the kingdom, then it is in the best interest of the churches to re-establish rigorous ordination programs which can, over time, offer a clear picture of a man in every area of his life and ministry. In the next chapter a model of ordination is presented which, while intended to be used as it stands, can be adapted to fit any denominational or ecclesiastical situation.

PART 2

Introduction

In the first part of this book we have looked broadly at the matter of ordination and described it as the public affirmation by the church of God's personal appointment of a man to be His herald in the church. Now it is time to take a closer look at the process.

In many ways, the ordination process is like a good tool. Growing up I was blessed by God to have a father who loved tools, and knew how to use them. Quite often as I watched Dad work he would take the time to explain just how a certain tool was to be used, and how it was perfectly suited to do a certain task. Ordination is a tool that accomplishes two things. First, it *critiques* a man, and everything about him, according to the standards God has set for pastoral ministry. In some ways, it is a ministerial X-ray through which the man must pass to determine the reality of God's call on his life. Secondly, it *charges* the man with the expectations of God Himself, and impresses upon him the grave responsibility he now carries. No ordination process is complete if it does not do both jobs.

Chapter 5 presents a general model for ordination that is particularly suited to my own denominational community of the Evangelical Free Church in America. However this does not mean that those with different ecclesiastical structures cannot use the material with benefit. What is at stake is the examination and affirmation of men claiming to have been appointed by God to pastoral ministry. The model presented, and the various parts of it, constitute one way of accomplishing the process. Those who find it necessary to adapt the model to fit their denominational practices will still find it to be a helpful basic blueprint for building an ordination process that brings glory to God, accountability to his ministers, and protection and provision to his church.

Chapter 6 is for the candidate and is meant to aid him in preparing for the various phases of the process. Chapter 7 gives suggestions for those serving on an ordination council and calls them to exercise their position in keeping with the seriousness of their task.

Chapter 5

The Process of Ordination

Growing up as a pastor's kid, I admit I eavesdropped on a fair amount of pastoral chitchat when area pastors would come by our home, or sit with our family at various pastoral retreats and conferences. I remember hearing about the usual successes and failures, the tough counseling problems, the new book or theological controversy, and always the latest 'pastors' jokes. And I also remember the ordination horror stories. Sometimes they came from men who made their ordination experiences sound like that of a young boy being harassed by school-yard bullies. Others showed their envy for those men whose connections had allowed them to come before an ordination council stacked with sympathetic friends, relatives and former teachers. As I have come to realize, either way the process failed both the church and the man.

Today, things have not changed. Ask around and you will soon find a pastor ready to tell you that his ordination process was either grossly unfair or greatly superficial, either a witch hunt or an Easter Egg hunt. While they may not be in the majority, far too many ordinations find their way to one of these extremes. It is my purpose in the second section of this book to present a model of ordination, along with suggestions for both the candidate and the council, that will keep the process from becoming either insensitive or insignificant. Such a process of ordination is characterized by expectations that are reasonable and clearly communicated, and is carried out knowing that God is the Judge to whom both candidate and council must answer for the seriousness and fairness with which they conduct themselves.

The process of ordination may be broken down into five phases: Personal Evaluation, Application and Licensure, Preparation, Formal Examination, and Deliberation and Affirmation.

Phase 1: Personal Evaluation

The starting place of every ordination process is the personal evaluation a man must make of himself. The initial stirrings of the Spirit in the heart that suggest that God may be calling him to enter pastoral ministry must be carefully evaluated. During this phase, which in some lives has taken years or even decades, the man needs to seek diligently all evidence that the desire he feels to pursue the ministry of pastoring is from God and not motivated by other concerns. It is important that the man not move to the next phase of the process until he is reasonably sure that God is calling him to pastoral ministry. This does not mean that he will have no doubts about his calling and fitness. Indeed, the humility required to be God's herald will display itself in a righteous sense of inadequacy that is neither false modesty nor cowardice. And yet, in the lives of those he calls, God builds a confidence, not in their own adequacy, but in the adequacy of God. Paul sums it up in 2 Corinthians 3:4-6:

> And such confidence we have through Christ toward God. Not that we are adequate in ourselves to consider anything as coming from ourselves, but our adequacy is from God, who also made us adequate as servants of a new covenant ...

This God-formed mixture of personal reticence and divine confidence, poured into the man's heart from the time of his internal call, must continue to characterize both his person and ministry throughout his years of service. For the man striving to determine the reality of God's call on his life, this is the place to begin his evaluation: *Am I both terrified and thrilled at the prospect of serving as God's herald?* But this is only the beginning.

As a man evaluates the reality of God's call on his life he must consider three areas. First, he must come to understand the seriousness of the pastoral task and do the investigation necessary to understand the realities of pastoral ministry. Secondly, he must measure himself against God's standards for ministry previously discussed: Desire, Character, Message, and Gifts. Lastly, he must recognize that there is nobility in *not* pursuing ordination if there are reasons to believe that God has not called him to that purpose.

1. The Seriousness of the Pastoral Task

Several years ago, at a meeting in Wheaton, Illinois, of the Whitefield Ministerial Fraternal, Alistair Begg offered the following quote from the mind of Bruce Thielman:

> The pulpit calls those anointed to it as the sea calls its sailors. And like the sea it batters and bruises and does not rest. To preach, to really preach is to die naked a little at a time, and to know each time you do it that you're going to have to do it again.[1]

Perhaps not as drastic but every bit as telling, was this comment from a friend upon hearing that I had been granted ordination. He said, 'Congratulations...now you get to wash between the toes!' At the time it struck me as odd, but since that day I have considered that he expressed a very necessary sentiment. *Ordained ministry is a serious*

---

[1]   Quoted from The Pulpit: Its Power and Pitfalls, a lecture delivered by Rev. Alistair Begg, at the Whitefield Ministerial Fraternal, Wheaton, Illinois, 1993.

*and strenuous calling that requires from a man a radical refusal
to set any limits on what God may demand of him.*

Any man considering ordination must heed the
words of Jesus himself. In John 13:16, after graphically
illustrating the posture of true leadership by washing his
disciples' feet, Jesus reminded these men that 'a slave is
not greater than his master; neither is one who is sent
greater than the one who sent him'. In so doing, Jesus
demonstrated that those who are sent as God's heralds
must see their task as modeling the task of Jesus, the
great Herald of God. The pastoral ministry is not merely
a profession in which a man may use his creative abilities
to gain a following. It is a divine calling to follow in the
footsteps of Christ, to declare a message once and for all
delivered, to labor for the Light in a world that prefers
darkness, and all the time consider it a grand privilege
to have been entrusted with the ministry of the gospel.

What is necessary for every man, when he begins
to feel the emotional stirrings of a desire to preach and
pastor, is to count the cost. In describing the true disciple,
Jesus likened it to a man desiring to build a tower: 'For
which of you, when he wants to build a tower, does
not first sit down and calculate the cost, to see if he has
enough to complete it?' (Luke 14:28f.). Many men enter
pastoral ministry unable to answer this question because
they have never really taken the time to 'calculate the
cost'.

Any man looking into pastoral ministry would do
well to read widely on the subject, and do some interviews with pastors to gain insight into the pastoral task
and challenges. Short-term ministry opportunities and
internships are also helpful in allowing a man to assess
the challenges and responsibilities of ministry. And perhaps most important, he must get insights on his ministerial fitness from as many careful observers as he can.

2. *The Standards Demanded*

Not only must a man calculate the cost, he must determine if he has what the task will demand. A big part of 'Phase 1: Personal Evaluation' is asking yourself the tough questions: *Do you have reasonable grounds to believe that God is drafting you for his service, and that he is even now fitting you with the necessary desire, character, knowledge and gifts to fulfil the ministry he will entrust to you?* The answer to this question calls for an unbiased appraisal of your life as measured by the standards God has set. These have already been discussed in chapters three and four and need not be reviewed here. But what is necessary here is to stress that while it is not reasonable to suggest that a man just beginning to sense the call of God will be exemplary already, it is essential that the first fruits of what God demands be evident in his life. The following questions will prove helpful:

- Do I see evidence of the Spirit of God in my life? Are there things in my life for which I can find no other explanation than the presence of the Spirit of God? Does my life testify that I have been born again to eternal life?

- Does my character suggest that God is fitting me for pastoral ministry? Am I alarmed when reading 1 Timothy 3 and Titus 1 that there are areas of my life that are radically out of sync with what God demands of a spiritual leader? Am I making progress in the area of character, and do I long to rid my life of those habits and attitudes that keep me from displaying consistent Christian character?

- Are my motives pure in seeking to enter ministry? Am I already involved in the ministry of the gospel in some way, and does it fill my heart with joy? Am I honest with myself and with others about the true motives of my heart for pursuing ordained ministry? Am I willing to rid my life and heart of those things that will keep me from loving the life of a servant?

- Do I love God's Word? Am I reasonably knowledgeable about Scripture and the doctrines of the Christian faith? Does my desire to teach the Word to others spring from the joy I've experienced as it has transformed my life? Am I growing in my ability to express the truth of God in a winsome and loving way?

- Do I show the first signs of the necessary ministerial gifts? Do I have a heart for people, and a mind capable of knowing and communicating God's word to them? Do I like to study? Do I appreciate prayer? Do I have a realistic appraisal of my abilities that is neither arrogant nor cowardly?

As you ask yourself these questions it is also important to widen your circle of critique to include those men under whom God has placed you for spiritual oversight. Certainly this should include your pastor and elders as well as other godly men in your life. If married, be sure to listen to your wife's perspective on your life as well. It is extremely important that, as you begin this process, you learn to tell yourself the truth about yourself, and that you discipline yourself to hear and acknowledge others when they speak the truth to you.

At this point a word also needs to be said regarding the importance of theological training. As we have seen, what the Bible requires for pastoral ministry is adequate biblical knowledge, theological reflection, and ministerial skills. What was not explicitly stated is the way such knowledge and skills are to be gained. History is full of examples of men who never attended religious school or seminary and yet enjoyed God's blessing on their ministries. And yet none of them would deny that there is great benefit gained from completion of a systematic and supervised course of theological instruction. While there may be notable exceptions, by far the normal and usual way that God prepares a man for pastoral leadership is through formal theological education under the supervision of gifted instructors in a recognized and respected college or seminary. This is not to say that the knowledge gained at such a school is all that is needed! Personally, I have found that my ability to shepherd the flock of God is vitally dependent upon a rigorous ongoing program of reading and self-education. But it is the knowledge and skills I gained at seminary that put me in a position to interact with, and benefit from, the material available today. In a very real sense, formal theological training is both the product I left with at graduation, and the engine that moves me forward in the quest for greater insight today.

3. The Nobility of not Pursuing Ordination

When I was a child I heard my father say, 'If God has called you to preach, don't step down to be the President of the United States. But if your heart will let you do anything besides preaching, do it!' Now I am sure that my dad was not the first to say it that way, for every man whom God has called has understood and expressed the same thing in some way. The calling of God to preach and pastor is a high calling which brings great satisfaction despite the challenges, frustrations, hardships, and toil; but those who enter pastoral ministry apart from the genuine call of God find it to be among the most frustrating and miserable employment situations ever, with little joy and even less sense of accomplishment.

During this beginning phase of the ordination process a man must recognize that it is noble to recognize the fact that God is not really calling him to pastoral ministry. If, during the course of investigation and personal evaluation, he comes to see that the task would overwhelm his areas of weakness, or that his desire is not from God, he must consider it the path of obedience *not* to pursue ordained ministry. Doing so may mean going against the wishes and dreams of others, and perhaps even his own. Nevertheless, for the good of the church and for the progress of his own soul, he must graciously agree with God that he is better suited for ministry outside the office of pastor.

In summary, Phase 1 is the time for the man to determine the real nature of pastoral ministry, and evaluate his own personal fitness for the task. In soliciting the honest views of spiritual advisors, and asking tough questions of himself, he may find that there is every reason to believe that God is calling him to pastoral ministry. Now he is ready to begin Phase 2.

Phase 2: Application and Licensure
This phase consists of two parts: Application and the First Council Examination.

Application
The first step after completing Phase 1 is to make official application to the ordaining body of your church organization. Upon receiving notice that you desire to pursue ordination, you will be given an Application Packet containing:

- Application for Ordination: This form asks for basic personal information, educational background, ministry experience, character and ministry references, and an affirmation that you are in agreement with the doctrinal standards of the organization.

- Instructions: This includes an Overview of the Ordination Process, a Timeline of the process, and a written Statement of Expectations, giving the candidate the policies, expectations, and requirements for completing the whole ordination process.

The First Council Examination

After the Application is completed and returned, the information is given to the Ordination Council. This council consists of those men entrusted by the organization to oversee the ordination process. Using the information on the Application, the council will gather information regarding the candidate's conversion, character, attitude toward ministry, ministry gifts, and over-all ministry fitness. If, in the council's opinion, the candidate is not ready to pursue ordination, they will inform him and the process will end. If the council is convinced that the candidate meets all the requirements, they will inform him that his application has been accepted and set a date for the candidate to sit for the First Council Examination.

This examination, often called a Licensure Examination, is much more limited than the Second, or Ordination, Examination. This First Council Examination is called specifically to:

- affirm the candidate's conversion

- examine his character according to biblical standards

- determine his motives for pursuing ordination

- affirm that his basic doctrinal beliefs are in line with the organization's standards

- consider his ministry experience and the evidence that he displays some ministerial gifts.

This examination deals primarily with the man rather than with his doctrinal beliefs and biblical knowledge. While the council certainly will ask that the man affirm his agreement with the doctrinal position of the organization, this is not the place for full, theological examination. Rather, the purpose of this first examination is to decide if the man's life gives evidence that God may indeed be calling him into pastoral ministry. As with all the various steps of the ordination process, failure here will stop the process.

Upon successful completion of this First Council Examination, the organization confers upon the candidate a License for Christian Ministry. This license does two things: it designates the man as fit to act in ministry in the church, and it gives public notice to the church that this man desires to be evaluated by the church over time in order to determine if God has called him to pastoral ministry. This license brings the man into full candidacy for ordination and does not reflect anything more than the decision of the council that this man is being considered for full ordination. With this license, the man may perform all pastoral functions, under the oversight of ordained staff, for the period of at least a year, and usually no more than three.

Phase 3: Preparation

During the time of the candidate's Licensure, he is involved in three important areas:

1) Mentor Assisted Study

With the conferral of License, the council will also assign a mentor to work with the candidate during his preparation for full ordination. This works best when the mentor is on the pastoral team of the candidate's church. The mentor's task is to assist the candidate in designing a course of self-study that will lead to the writing of the candidate's Doctrinal Position Paper, and a successful completion of the Second Council Examination. Not only does this help the candidate in the process, but the assignment of a mentor places an ordained man in a favorable position to comment later on the candidate's spirituality, character, gifts and overall fitness for ordination. Given that the mentor plays such an important role in the process, it is best if potential mentors be recognized and affirmed by the council, and given prior instructions regarding their role and task.

During his time of Licensure, the candidate must study hard to make sure that he has a broad and con-sistent understanding of Scripture and doctrine, and can articulate his views and defend them.

2) Doctrinal Position Paper

During the years of Licensure the candidate will be writing his personal position paper describing and defending his theological views, and demonstrating that he is not only in agreement with the organization's doctrinal standards, but also understands the complexities of the theological world and can defend biblical orthodoxy using Scripture. This written paper must be complete and detailed, covering aspects of practical theology and Christian living as well, in accordance with the published expectations of the ordination council.

3) Church Ministry

The candidate is involved in church ministry in a variety of settings, under the supervision of his pastoral mentor. This allows for ongoing evaluation of his ministerial gifts and attitude.

During this time of Licensure, the process will be greatly helped if the mentor maintains some communication with the ordaining council. It is also extremely important that the members of the council attend one or more services where the candidate is teaching or preaching. Short of this, taped copies of sermons or lessons can allow the council to evaluate the candidate's progress in ministering the word.

After a minimum of one full year, and when the candidate has completed his Doctrinal Position Paper to the satisfaction of the mentor, and with the mentor's recommendation, the council will set a date for the Second Examination Council. Three months before that date, the candidate will distribute his position paper to each of the council members. Prior to the council date, the council members will review the paper, communicate with the mentor regarding the candidate's character and ministry, and evaluate examples of his teaching.

It is very important that the council do their work prior to the Second Examination Council. They must study the paper, especially to see if it demonstrates the necessary understanding of doctrinal issues. If, in the opinion of the council, the paper does not show that the candidate is ready to sit for oral examination, the process must be terminated and the candidate asked to wait at least one year before submitting another paper. Notice I do not say postpone the examination. Failure to produce a credible paper must be seen as a reason to deny the candidate entrance into the next phase, and instead extend Phase 3 of the ordination process.

It is critical to understand that the purpose of the ordination process is *not* to help men get into pastoral ministry. Rather, it is to affirm those men whom God has already called and equipped. When the evidence of God's call is lacking, it is not the place of the council to help the candidate over the challenges. The council must resist the temptation to become a group of tutors who help navigate unqualified candidates through the rapids of the ordination process, for this goes against their very core purpose for existing. Candidates who do not submit acceptable papers must be sent back to their books for further study and training. It may very well be that those who cannot articulate and defend their beliefs properly were never drafted by God in the first place. If, after repeated attempts, a candidate is unable to present an acceptable paper, it is to be determined that the man is not truly a candidate for ordination, and his license must be revoked.

When the council decides, after reviewing the candidate's paper and other pertinent information, that the candidate is ready, the process will proceed to Phase 4: The Second Council Examination.

Phase 4: The Second Council Examination

This council examination consists of a day-long opportunity for the candidate to present his theological views and answer the questions of the council. This examination is a serious attempt to determine the breadth of the candidate's biblical knowledge, the consistency and orthodoxy of his theological knowledge, and his ability to define, defend, and describe it all using Scripture.

In addition to the candidate, the council will also want to hear from the candidate's spouse, mentor, and others who have had the opportunity to observe his character and sit under his ministry.

Phase 5: Deliberation and Affirmation

Following the Second Council Examination, the council should take sufficient time to deliberate together and review the questions and answers given. The seriousness of the task must take precedence over convenience, and at times, the deliberations may not be completed on the same day as the examination. Suggestions for keeping the examination and deliberation fair and objective are given in a later chapter.

The decision of the council should be communicated to the candidate within a week, and preparations should begin immediately for the public affirmation of successful candidates. This public affirmation should be held in the church where the candidate serves, and bring together both the council and the church in a final affirmation of God's calling on the man.

6

Preparing for Ordination[1]

As a father in America today, one of my greatest enjoyments has been coaching my children as they participated in youth sports. And as a coach, I learned many important lessons that have served me well in church life. One of them is this: *it was often the case that the most talented players on the team also were the ones who practised the hardest.* They were the ones who wanted to practice because they truly loved the game. They came early and stayed late, always wanting to throw a little more, or kick the ball a few more times. Their love for the sport translated into a love for all the little parts of the sport, and was all the motivation they needed to do those things that made them even better.

On the other hand, there were those kids who wanted to play in the game, but really had no time for practice. Usually they were the ones who needed the practice, and their lack of practice always showed itself on game day. What it all boiled down to was this: *they wanted to be successful on game day, but they really didn't love the sport.* Loving the sport means enjoying the little parts of the sport that make up the practice session. Loving soccer really means enjoying kicking the ball, dribbling, passing, shooting, and it makes no difference whether it is in practice or a match. Kids who love baseball love to

---

1   (This chapter is written for those who, having been granted ministerial license, are now preparing themselves for the Second Ordination
Exam.)

play catch, hit the ball, and are famous for saying to their dads, 'Just ten more grounders, please?'

My point is this: as you prepare for ordination, recognize that the next few years will provide you with a wonderful opportunity to see if you really love the game or merely want to be successful on game day. Preparation for ordination is very similar to the pastoral task, and to be truly successful and satisfied, you must genuinely love the little parts that make up the whole. Do you love to talk about Jesus? Do you love to read and reflect on theological subjects? Do you love to study, and write, and sharpen your ideas on the iron of other men's convictions? Are you in love with God's Word and enjoy digging deeply into its limitless treasures? Do you love to pray, pouring your heart out to God? Do you love to be with people in need? Do you love to meet new people and see them as opportunities to herald the truth of Christ? Do not expect that you will ever be a good pastor if you do not love the little parts of the pastoral task. On the other hand, if you love the game, if you love to read and study and speak and serve, your diligence during the months of preparation for the Second Ordination Exam will stand you in good stead on exam day, and will testify to the reality of God's call on your life.

The time between Licensure and the ordination examination should be used to concentrate on the following areas: personal study, personal appraisal, pastoral service, mentor appraisal, doctrinal paper preparation, and preparation for the Second Ordination Exam.

Personal Study
Having given notice to the church through Licensure that you are intentional in your pursuit of ordination, it becomes all the more necessary to pursue the knowledge needed for pastoral ministry. From Paul's instructions to Titus to find men who can 'both instruct in sound doctrine

and refute those who are in opposition' (Titus 1:9), it is clear that it takes a certain level of biblical, theological, and practical knowledge to be successful in pastoral ministry. Those who have completed college and/or seminary training certainly have an advantage, although every pastor has been known to exclaim, 'They never taught me this in school!' The time between Licensure and ordination should be used to:

> **read** in the areas of biblical studies, theology, and practical theology, including staying current on the popular issues of the day through the use of journals. Take the opportunity to read, especially in those areas where your knowledge is lacking, and in those areas that you will cover in your Doctrinal Position Paper. Many denominations have a list of required reading for their ordination candidates. Be sure to include them in your reading plan. Ask your mentor to suggest books and articles as well. The statement 'readers are leaders' seems particularly applicable to successful, faithful pastoral ministry.

> **write** short position papers on theological and practical issues. This will help you focus your views, and provide the basis for the various sections of the Doctrinal Position Paper.

> **reflect** on your reading and written views with your mentor. Conversations with your mentor will provide opportunity for you to verbally describe and defend your positions. This not only allows him to help you form and reform your views, but also gives you practice in stating and defending your convictions.

Personal Appraisal

In his instructions to Timothy, Paul wrote, 'Pay close attention to yourself, and to your teaching; persevere in these things; for as you do this you will ensure salvation both for yourself and for those who hear you' (1 Tim. 4:16). Throughout the life of God's herald he must ever be keeping a close and critical eye on himself to make sure that his heart is not growing cold toward God and his truth. As you prepare for ordination, develop the habit of personal appraisal. Ask yourself the tough questions and be honest in your answers, for more is at stake than your personal well-being. If you are granted ordination the welfare of a church will become largely dependent upon you. And while we all have seen the disastrous results of the pastor who has disqualified himself, the consequences are only slightly less grave in the case of a pastor who was unqualified from the start. If God is appointing you, it will be evident in your life, your love, your leadership ability, and your progress in the gifts and graces of ministry. But if, as you prepare for ordination, you find that your heart is not in it, or that your desires are not in step with those of the kingdom of Christ, or that the essential attitudes and abilities of ministry are lacking, be righteous in your self-appraisal and admit that God's call on your life is not to the task of pastoral ministry.

Pastoral Service

Having been granted a ministerial license, you are now able to participate in pastoral ministry under the oversight of your mentor, and others of your pastoral team. Take advantage of it! Pour yourself into every ministry opportunity you are given, and seek ways to participate in a wide variety of pastoral tasks. These include teaching and preaching, counseling, leadership meetings, missions committee meetings, hospital and home visitations, personal evangelism, worship planning, music, crisis counseling and intervention, funerals, weddings, children and youth ministries, teaching and administration of the sacraments. This wide exposure offers two advantages: (1) it allows you to experience the reality of pastoral ministry to see if you have the stuff to do the job; (2) it allows your mentor to see you in a variety of ministry situations and offer insight, encouragement, and corrective counsel.

Mentor Appraisal

As you study and serve, it is vital to gain your mentor's perspective on your life and ministry. In addition to the unofficial time you spend together, be sure there are set times each month when you listen to his critique and suggestions in the areas of your personal and family life, spiritual disciplines, interaction with people, biblical and theological thought, and communicating God's Word. Gain his insight by asking questions such as:

- *Where do you see God's hand most noticeably in my life and ministry?*

- *What areas of weakness continue to surface?*

- *How would you evaluate my progress:*

    - *in dealing with people?*

    - *in study and preparation to teach?*

    - *in public communication of the Word?*

    - *in making ministry and leadership decisions?*

    - *in helping those involved in conflict?*

    - *in helping those who are suffering?*

    - *in dealing with those who oppose and disagree?*

    - *in responding to the suggestions of others?*

- *What is your perspective on the health of my marriage and my family?*

- *How would you evaluate my use of the Bible, and over-all theological comprehension?*

As you prepare for ordination recognize that the life-on-life instruction you gain from your mentor is every bit as important as the knowledge gained from your personal study. Your interaction with him will sharpen you in practical areas and help fit you not only to complete the ordination process successfully, but to minister effectively as God's herald to the world.

Writing the Doctrinal Position Paper (DPP)

Over the years I have served on ordination councils I have read many DPPs. Often the paper is my first introduction to the candidate, and the paper creates the impression of the candidate that I bring with me to the ordination exam. Some men use the DPP well, describing and defending their views systematically, clearly, simply, and yet with necessary completeness. Others appear to think of their papers as reformational documents that will one day be tacked to a village church door. Still other men use their papers to get the council to think the author knows more than he does. These men fill their papers with obscure terms and quotes, and usually end up red-faced on examination day. As the ordination proceeds toward the final ordination examination, their preliminary thoughts of the candidate and his beliefs are largely shaped by the DPP. Consequently, the time and effort you put into writing a good paper – one that accurately reflects your convictions and adequately defends them, and is written in a sincere and competent style – will be rewarded on examination day. The following general suggestions for writing the DPP are meant to be used alongside those instructions given to you by the ordination council or ordaining body.

(1) Be sure the DPP is a reflection of you. The purpose is to reflect your study, your convictions, your style, your ability to use Scripture. Use words and a writing style that you can own and that accurately reflect what you know and how you think.

- Don't make the mistake of using other men's words to express your beliefs; they are not being examined, you are.

- Don't adopt a writing style that is at odds with who you really are. Use only terms and concepts that you understand and can adequately define and defend. As well, be careful not to adopt an overly scholarly tone. It is my experience that ordination councils tend to challenge more strongly those men whose papers evidence that the author has a high opinion of his own scholarship and insight. Be aware that if you make yourself sound like a seminary professor, the council will expect you to demonstrate that level of competence.

(2) Be sure the DPP is complete. There is a difference between being exhaustive and being complete. Being exhaustive means touching on every possible subject; being complete means touching on every necessary subject. As an example, take the doctrine of the atonement. An exhaustive paper would present every view of the atonement, along with material designed to prove or disprove it. A complete paper would present your view of the atonement, along with all the necessary parts of it (substitution, redemption, extent, propitiation, effect, etc.), using proper theological and biblical arguments. Of course, in your defence before the council, it is essential that you be familiar with views other than your own so that you can defend your view against them, and cite the biblical reasons why, in your opinion, they must bow to yours. The paper is not the place for debate; rather, the paper is to describe and defend your position clearly and completely.

Also in the area of being complete, be sure not to exclude any necessary parts of the various doctrines you will cover. For example, in describing their view of

Scripture, many men do a good job defending their views of inspiration and authority, but leave out almost entirely any discussion of the important area of canonicity. One of the greatest areas of weakness in DPPs is that they leave out essential aspects of doctrinal study.

Writing a DPP that is complete will take time. Don't assume that it can be written all at once over a few days. Rather, following the instructions of the ordaining body regarding the DPP, and using the ongoing input of your mentor as you write the various sections of the paper, you will be able to form and reform your paper so that it is consistent and complete.

(3) Be sure that your paper demonstrates that you understand the complexity of the various theological mysteries and that, in response, you have done the work to come to a position that you can now hold with confidence. It is not uncommon for young theologians especially to present their view as the only one anyone with any smarts would hold! Such a stand demonstrates a shallow understanding of the true complexities of the subject. For example, take the discussion on the extent of the atonement. Regardless of which side you defend (unlimited against particular redemption), it is necessary to admit that there are challenging texts with which both sides must deal fairly. The careful Calvinist must deal fairly and clearly with 1 John 2:2, and the careful Arminian must speak directly to the challenges of 2 Corinthians 5:19. Another more contemporary example relates to the role of women in the church. The careful biblical exegete must not only camp in 1 Timothy 2:12, 13 but must also deal fairly and completely with Galatians 3:28. The point is just this: the kind of mature, theological reflection necessary for pastoral ministry is seen in understanding that sincere, godly people hold views the opposite to yours for some apparently good reasons. Not to acknowledge that, or to present your

views as though only fools would hold something else, demonstrates a lack of deep theological reflection. While it is clear that differing opinions cannot both be right, it is equally clear that the theological debates that have raged for centuries will never be settled if we refuse to acknowledge the areas of valid concern both camps are trying to raise. As a candidate for ordination it is essential that, even as you define and defend your own view, you demonstrate a healthy and honorable knowledge of both the strengths and weaknesses of opposing views. While it is not necessary to describe opposing views, the way in which you present your view will show the degree to which you have wrestled with them.

(4) Be sure to use Scripture wisely and properly in defining and defending your views. Don't assume that by simply citing a reference, the council will understand the text to be supporting what you affirm. If you use the proof text method, be ready to describe how each text fits into its context, and how it fits into your argument. Be doubly sure that you are citing the right text, and that your interpretation and use of the text is legitimate. Where possible, use a paragraph of text to support your view, rather than several separated and isolated texts.

One of the prime ways a council examines a candidate is to ask him to explain how a certain text in the paper supports the view under consideration. This is especially true of texts that are supposed to be standard texts. For example, every DPP I have ever read uses 2 Timothy 3:16, 17 to support the doctrine of inspiration. But when a wily council member asks the candidates how Paul's statement here regarding the Scriptures of the day – the Old Testament – relates to the inspiration of the New Testament, they often find themselves scrambling for answers. The point is this: when you cite a biblical reference be sure you really understand how it fits, and be ready to express it if questioned.

(5) Be aware that everything you write becomes fair game for questions from the council. I will never forget the time one candidate quoted Augustine in his paper. During the examination, one council member began quizzing the candidate about Augustine's view of the church, effectively calling the candidate to demonstrate his knowledge of Augustine's writings. When, in only seconds, it became apparent that the quote represented the extent of his 'Augustinian expertise', the point was made. Another example was a candidate who, in discussing the nature of man, incorporated some philosophical terms and concepts from Plato and others. Again, when one of the council members who was particularly well trained in philosophy began probing him in the area of Neo-Platonism, it was quickly seen that the candidate was not a true student of philosophy. What can you learn from this? Be careful to write only that which you can confidently define and defend.

(6) Remember that the DPP is to be a straightforward presentation of your views in the particular areas of theology and practice asked for by the ordaining body. It is not a sermon, or a Sunday School curriculum. It is not to be a polemic designed to change the views of the council or the church. It is not the place for personal testimonials, illustrations, humor, misrepresentation of opponents, famous quotations, footnotes, or poetry. In particular, be careful how you use theological clichés or catch phrases. Many a candidate has crashed on the rocks when asked to explain a cliché or phrase that, in his mind, was so standard that he had never taken the time to reflect on what it really meant. For example, I always ask men to define what they mean by justification by faith. It is amazing how many men fumble around with the answer because they have so long assumed the statement of the doctrine (Justification by Faith) to be the definition of it as well. It is only when they get around

to defining it correctly as 'justification by grace alone through faith alone in Christ alone' that they get back on track. The wise candidate won't ever assume that the standard theological phrases and formulas he puts in his paper will be understood by the council and taken at face value. He will be certain that, if asked, he can define and defend even the most common theological terms.

(7) Lastly, present your positions with confidence but not arrogance. Do the work necessary to take a stand on a position. Then hold to it firmly, using Scripture as the foundation. But do so with the understanding that it is never honorable to uphold error and, if convinced by the Word, you would gladly adopt a more truthful position. Be dogmatic both in your views and in your determination to ever be reforming your views according to Scripture. Such is the attitude of God's herald, and such is the attitude the council wants to see represented both in your paper and your examination.

Once your DPP is complete it should be reviewed by your mentor and approved. While mentor approval is certainly not a necessity, any concern expressed regarding the overall consistency and clarity of your paper should be taken seriously. When the paper is in its final form, and after having completed at least one year of mentor supervised pastoral ministry, you may contact the ordination council to arrange a date for your final ordination examination.

The Second Ordination Examination
The Second Ordination Examination provides the final test for the candidate. It also provides the most memorable part of the process for most candidates. Those who come well prepared, and demonstrate their competency with confidence and clarity, gain further assurance that God has indeed chosen them to lead and feed his flock. Consequently, those councils that challenge the candidate

the most, and do so in a fair and just way, end up providing the strongest affirmation to the candidate of his divine call. As you look forward to the examination recognize that every hour of preparation is an investment, not only in your ability to be affirmed by the council, but also in your future ministry of the Word in the church. Don't look for shortcuts, and don't aim merely to 'get by'. Aim high. Expect more of yourself than you believe the council will expect of you. Your greatest fear should not be that you will not pass. Your greatest fear must be that you will pass without having done the work to acquire a level of knowledge and insight indicative of God's call on your life.

During the Second Ordination Examination the council will be examining you to determine your fitness for pastoral ministry. In Part 1 we discussed the four broad areas in which God's man must be divinely crafted for the work: Desire, Character, Knowledge, and Gifts. While the examination will focus primarily on the area of Knowledge, the good council will also investigate the candidate's Desire and Character using both direct questions and written references. Usually consideration of the candidate's Gifts is done before the examination through the use of audio and video tapes, study outlines, and other examples of his teaching and preaching. As you look forward to your examination, the following suggestions will prove helpful.

Desire
Be prepared to explain your desire to enter pastoral ministry, and be careful to do so in a way that demonstrates the true motive of your heart. Are you truly willing to be a servant? Are you excited to serve the Lord, even if it means ministering in a small church in a small town for the duration of your ministry? Are you pursuing pastoral ministry because you have a driving passion for God's truth? Are you willing to spend the hours in study,

prayer, service, and discipline necessary for successful spiritual ministry? Do you love people? Ask yourself these questions and be brutally honest in your reflection and self-appraisal. As you formulate your answers, you are well on the way to preparing yourself to answer any questions the council may have regarding the reasons you are pursuing ordination, and their consistency with the servant's attitude described in Scripture.

Character

While the greatest evaluation of your character will come from your mentor's observation and other reference forms used by the council, you may be asked to describe areas in your life such as your marriage, your spiritual disciplines, your parenting style, your current economic health, your moral purity, and your customary way of dealing with opposition and conflict. But even more important than your answers to the council must be your honest appraisal of yourself in these areas. Can you honestly say that your character is exemplary in these areas? It must be firmly stated that we do not need any more pastors who are teetering on the brink of disaster in essential areas, and are afraid to admit it to themselves or others. The stakes are much higher than just your personal shame and humiliation. To enter ordained ministry knowing that areas of your life are out of control is to risk the wrath of God and the destruction of the church. As you prepare for your ordination examination, first be sure God approves of you. If your life enjoys his smile, the questions of the council will prove only to be an opportunity to testify to the grace and power of God in your life.

Knowledge

The greatest part of the ordination examination deals with the accumulated knowledge of the candidate. This knowledge is divided into three areas:

Biblical Knowledge: a comprehensive understanding of the Bible, its contents, themes, and difficulties. The candidate will be asked questions designed to see if he knows his Bible, and can use it in answering. While every council will have slightly different expectations (which should be published in the application packet), no candidate should enter the examination if he does not have the following:

- an understanding of the major themes of the individual books of the Bible

- an understanding of the great biblical themes, along with the ability to trace them through the Bible. For example: *What is the biblical understanding of 'covenant' and how would you briefly trace the concept through the Scripture?*

- a working knowledge of the contents of the Bible that is demonstrated in the ability to back up your answers with biblical texts, taken in their correct contexts.

Theological Knowledge: a comprehensive and consistent understanding of the doctrines presented in Scripture. Primarily, these are viewed using the standard divisions of Systematic Theology, and are presented in the Doctrinal Position Paper (DPP). You should be comfortable discussing the various challenges and controversies involved in theological study.

Pastoral Theology: a practical understanding of how the truth of God's Word defines the actions of the pastor in the various situations of pastoral ministry. You should be able to describe how you would handle various pastoral situations biblically. For example: *A woman in your church comes to you and admits that she is a lesbian, and is thinking of leaving her husband: how do you respond?*

General Suggestions

Generally speaking, the ordination examination should be your opportunity to show who you are theologically, and what you know biblically. It is important that you come to the examination confident in your knowledge and in your ability to communicate and defend your positions. While each candidate will have his own style and approach, here are a few general suggestions that will help put you in a position to do your best.

(1) Be so prepared that you can be relaxed during the examination. When I first started preaching my Dad commented that I should 'have the notes in my head, and not my head in the notes'. What he meant was that there is greater freedom to express your thoughts if you really know them, if they are a part of you. The same is true in the ordination examination. You will be most successful when your answers are an extension of who you are and what you know, rather than merely a re-telling of something you heard or read the previous night!

(2) Use Scripture often and well. Every question presents an opportunity to be God's herald. Support your answers with appropriate texts, using sections instead of single proof texts where possible. Be doubly sure that the texts you cite are used correctly, are consistent with the intention of the original author, and that you can back up your interpretation if challenged.

(3) Handle controversial subjects with both reflection and resolve. Councils use controversial subjects to critique candidates in two ways. First, the candidate's understanding of the issues and the relevant biblical material can be studied. But secondly, the council can watch to see how he will respond to those who may oppose his view. Be aware that a council member may even play the part of devil's advocate in arguing against you in order to find out how you respond to those with whom you

differ. The need in this situation is for both reflection and resolve. First, demonstrate that you have given careful reflection and study to the question posed. Demonstrate that you understand the complexities of the issue, the strengths and weaknesses of various viewpoints, and the sincerity of many who take opposing views. Secondly, present your view, based on Scripture, with resolve. Don't waffle in an attempt to please the council or one of its members. Above all, don't be drawn into a personal argument with a council member. Maintain your composure, admit the problems involved, retreat to Scripture, and calmly present your view.

(4) Ask questions where necessary to clarify just what you are being asked. If you don't understand the question, ask some of your own, and don't be afraid to jot down some notes as the council repeats the question.

(5) Take time to organize your answers. There is no rule that says you have to respond immediately to a question. In fact, taking 10-20 seconds to formulate an organized and complete answer shows the council that you do not respond off the top of your head. As you prepare to answer a question:

First, determine what textual section best speaks to the question and provides the foundation for your answer.

Second, jot down key words that stand for the main points you will cover.

Third, anticipate objections that will be raised by your answer, and consider how you will answer them if raised.

Last, know when you are done. Determine what your last point will be, what your last text will be, how you will finish the question. This will help keep you from having answers that run on and on giving the impression that you are scrambling for any answer that the council will accept.

(6) Be careful to distinguish your opinions from your convictions. This is especially important when you are asked to speak to issues which the Bible does not specifically address. For example, your ideas regarding social drinking, the legitimacy of taking out a mortgage, and whether or not a Christian should attend an 'R' rated movie, must be set in the context of opinion rather than biblical absolute. Let the council know that since the Scripture does not give specific direction, you are left to determine your course of action using wisdom. Then, state your view along with the reasons for it.

(7) Remember that you are being evaluated as a man claiming to have been appointed by God. As you answer the questions, do so in a way that demonstrates both your heart for truth and for people. Show how you would use certain truths to bring people closer to God, and how your answers ultimately point to the majesty of Christ. The greatest compliment you could receive from the council would be that your message and your manner was Christocentric.

7

The Ordination Council

While specific instruction on the activity of an ordination council is lacking in Scripture, there is clear indication that from the beginning of the apostolic period, the church has recognized the call of God on a man through the examination and affirmation by its leaders. Galatians 2:1-10 is Paul's own recounting of his examination and affirmation by the leaders of the Jerusalem church – Peter, James, and John. He reports that he 'submitted to them the gospel which I preach among the Gentiles, but I did so in private to those who were of reputation, for fear that I might be running, or had run, in vain' (v. 2). These men, 'seeing that I had been entrusted with the gospel to the uncircumcised' (v. 7) and 'recognizing the grace that had been given to me' (v. 9), gave to Paul and Barnabas 'the right hand of fellowship' (v. 9) and sent them on their way approved as heralds to the Gentile world. According to 1 Timothy 4:14 and 2 Timothy 1:6, Paul was involved in the latter affirmation of Timothy as he was appointed to preach the Word (see also 2 Tim. 4:1-4).

Today the ordination council functions as an arm of the church in overseeing the examination and affirmation of those men desiring to enter pastoral ministry. This chapter has two purposes. First, the function of the council must be understood as vitally important to the health of the church in that it provides the greatest safeguard against allowing unfit and dangerous men into positions of pastoral ministry. As such, those who serve on councils must see their task as a noble one, needing their best efforts, and worthy of the necessary investment of time and study. Secondly, the operation of the council during the whole process of ordination must exemplify the high standards God sets for those who serve him in positions of leadership. This chapter gives an overview of the areas in which the council must act and gives suggestions for doing so in an honorable, thorough, and fair way.

The Task of the Ordination Council

As stated, the task of the ordination council is not to see how many men they can affirm for pastoral ministry. To a great extent, it is just the opposite. The council must act to see that as few unqualified men as possible are granted ordination. To carry out their function well, the council must see its task as affirming what God has already done in the life of a man. They are called to examine a man and his message to see if there is reasonable evidence to conclude that God has called and crafted the man for pastoral ministry. Those whose character, desire, knowledge, and gifts testify to the call of God should be gladly affirmed. Those who do not measure up must not be affirmed, and this denial of affirmation must not be seen as a tragedy, for it actually fortifies the church. Every time an unqualified man is turned away, the purity of the pastorate is enhanced, and the health of the church protected. Given this great responsibility, those who serve on ordination councils must be diligent students of the process and must believe that what they are doing is serious business and fundamentally essential to the health and well-being of the church.

The Make-Up of the Council

Ideally the ordination council should be a standing committee comprised of ordained pastors currently ministering in local area churches. The texts cited above state that those who affirmed Paul and Timothy were recognized church leaders themselves. Allowing a group of pastors to remain as the ordination council for a geographical region has many advantages over those councils that are called together for single ordinations. The standing committee ensures that all candidates will be questioned and critiqued in roughly the same way, and that expectations and standards can be consistent from man to man. A council comprised of 5-8 men is best. Having less men risks letting the process be overly dominated by one or two, while having more usually means that there is not enough time for each man to ask his questions. Also, the larger the number of men on the council, the harder it is to schedule large blocks of time when all can attend.

Each council should designate a Chairman who will oversee the activity of the council, moderate the examinations, and handle correspondence with the candidates. Also, a council secretary should be assigned to take accurate notes of examination questions and answers. Lastly, each member of the council should be assigned to oversee the process of one or more individuals who have been granted Licensure. This task involves periodic conversations with the candidate's assigned mentor, initial reading of the completed Doctrinal Position Paper, and the sending and receiving of Character Reference forms and Teaching Response forms in anticipation of the Second Ordination Examination. This alleviates some of the Chairman's workload while keeping each council member vitally involved in the ordination process at the grassroots level.

Communicating with Candidates

One of the ways the ordination process can be kept honorable and respected is for the council to communicate with candidates in a timely, proactive, and clear way. It is important that candidates be treated as council members themselves would expect to be treated were the roles reversed.

(1) The Application Packet: Once a man has expressed his desire to pursue ordination, the council must send him an Application Packet that includes the following:

- Application for Ordination: this information-gathering form asks the candidate for appropriate personal, educational, and ministry information, including names of character references.

- Ordination Process Overview and Timeline: this walks the candidate through the entire process, carefully summarizing what each phase of the process is designed to do. This includes information on who to contact with questions, and how to let the council know when it is time to schedule the Second Ordination Examination.

- Expectations: in the Application Packet, the council should include a thorough explanation of the standards by which the candidate will be judged.

(This book, in part or as a whole, would provide the candidate with an excellent overview of both the process of ordination, and the expectations of the council.)

(2) Correspondence: Throughout the process, individuals on the council will be corresponding with the candidate, answering questions, informing him of their decisions, and offering counsel, among other things. It is important that such communication be done in a timely manner, and that written copies be kept to avoid future misunderstandings.

Setting Standards for Examinations
One of the greatest areas of discouragement in my time on ordination councils has been the almost universal agreement not to judge every candidate according to the

same standard. Councils can be easy one day and almost mean-spirited the next, depending on how they are feeling. Individuals on the council, left to their own systems of adjudication, sometimes let their own mood or their initial impression of the candidate dictate their appraisal of him. Worst of all, some council members pick one or two doctrinal positions, or character traits, and determine a candidate's fitness based only on his performance in those areas. What is needed to prevent the examination from becoming capricious is a mutually agreed standard of expectation and examination. The expectations must be formulated by the council, in keeping with denominational dictates, and then clearly communicated to candidates. To allow for consistent examination and scoring, the following standardized scoring system is suggested.

Standardized Scoring System:
Both of the ordination exams (Licensure and the final examination) should be broken down into four broad areas: Knowledge, Character, Desire, and Gifts. The Knowledge area should be further divided into Theological Knowledge, Biblical Knowledge, and Pastoral Theology. For each section, the candidate should be rated on a four-point scale. The three areas of Knowledge should be averaged to give the overall Knowledge score. An example of such a scoring system is given on the next page:

	Unacceptable	Acceptable	Good	Excellent
Knowledge				
Theological	1	2	3	4
Biblical	1	2	3	4
Pastoral	1	2	3	4
Character	1	2	3	4
Desire/Attitude	1	2	3	4
Gifts	1	2	3	4

For each of the areas, the individual council members would rate the candidate privately, adding the scores for the four main areas together to give a final score for each candidate. The scores of each council member would be averaged to get an overall council rating. A 1 rating in any area by the combined council would be an automatic reason for rejecting the candidate. A score of 8-9, while reflecting acceptable performance, would necessitate extended discussion by the council to see if the man should be affirmed. A score of 10 and higher would be seen as suggesting affirmation by the council. Where there was wide disagreement between council members, extended discussion would be necessary to reach agreement.

This simple scoring system, besides bringing some objectivity to the process, also directs the council to examine all the important areas, rather than major only on one or two. Also, it must be recognized that certain questions posed to the candidate give the opportunity for him to be examined in more than one area. For example, a question on how to handle a couple in the church who are considering divorce would give insight into the candidate's theological views on divorce, his biblical knowledge of divorce texts, and his pastoral theology regarding dealing with the issue. It could also give insight into his attitude of ministry (is he harsh or gentle?).

Lastly, use of a scoring method provides objective answers should a candidate be rejected and want to know why. Instead of offering general reasons, the Chairman could consult the scoring sheets to see the specific areas in which the candidate was found lacking.

Gathering Information on the Candidate

Once a man has asked to be considered for ordination, and has returned the Application for Ordination, the council must assign him to one of the council members. The council member then begins the task of acquiring basic information regarding the candidate's character and fitness for potential ministry. He should first contact the candidate's pastor to see if he is in agreement with the candidate's request for ordination. Then he must use the following forms to gain further information about the candidate:

Character Reference Form: this form should be simple, and directed at five believers who have access to the candidate's life and ministry. They should be asked to comment on his overall character, marriage, family, etc. They should also be asked to describe anything about the candidate that they feel would either disqualify him from ministry or hinder his successful completion of the ordination process.

Teaching Response Form: this form should be designed to allow those who sit under the candidate's ministry to adjudicate his ability to teach and minister in the area of the Word.

Both of these forms should be received back to the council prior to setting a date for Licensure examination. If, on the basis of the material acquired, the council determines that he is not ready even to start the process, they must communicate this to him clearly, informing him that he will have to wait at least a year before reapplying for ordination.

The First Council Examination

As mentioned previously, the First Council Examination is called for the simple purpose of affirming the man's basic fitness for ministry, as described in chapter 5. This is not to be an extensive theological examination but rather an honest examination of the man. At this council examination it is helpful to have the candidate's pastor, spouse, and one or two acquaintances attend with him. After questioning the candidate, he can be dismissed while questions regarding his life and ministry are addressed to them. It is best at this stage of the process to limit the participants to the council, the candidate, and those accompanying him at the request of the council. This examination is not a public affair. Below are some sample questions for use in examining the basic areas of a man's life and message:

Conversion

- Describe your conversion.

- If you were to die right now, and God were to ask you why He should allow you into heaven, what would you say?

- Describe the changes that have occurred in your life since God granted you forgiveness of sins.

- Describe the feelings of remorse and repentance that you had when the Spirit brought you conviction of sin.

Character

- How would you rate yourself on a scale of 1-10 for each of the qualifications given in 1 Timothy 3 and Titus 1, with 10 being exceptional and 1 being dismal?

- In what areas of personality and character have you seen the most improvement since God saved you?

- In what areas of personality and character do you most find yourself needing to improve?

- How do you feel about your life becoming a display model of what someone's life will become if they trust the Jesus you preach?

- Is there anything in your life that would bring shame to you, the church , or the testimony of Christ, if it became known publicly?

- Are you currently involved, or have you ever been involved, with unholy habits such as sexual immorality, pornography, use of illegal drugs, etc.?

- Is the status of your married life up to God's standard?

- Are you a godly father?

- Are your finances in order, and do they testify to the fact that you are a wise man, in control of your life, and not driven by greed or materialism?

Desire

- Give us your view of how God's leaders ought to see themselves.

- What do you understand by the term 'servant leadership' and what does it look like in the life of a pastor?

- Which of the following do you think best describes the pastor: (you can choose more than one)

  · Leader   · Manager   · Helper
  · CEO   · Shepherd   · Teacher
  · Parent   · President · General

- What will it look like for you when you are 'successful' in ministry?

- Describe your ideal ministerial setting.

- Who is your favorite leader in the Bible, other than Christ? Why?

- Who today, in your opinion, best typifies what a pastor ought to be in our country?

Gifts

- What do you believe your primary areas of giftedness are? Why?

- Where have you used your gifts? In what capacities? What was the response?

- How have you worked to improve your gifts of teaching and preaching?

- What education have you completed that will help you in the tasks of pastoral ministry?

- What has brought you to the place that you believe God is calling you into the ordained public ministry?

Doctrine

- Do you understand and agree with the doctrinal statement of our church and/or denomination?

- Are there any areas where you are reluctant to give full agreement? What are they, and why?

Assigning a Mentor

Once a candidate has been granted Licensure, the council must assign him a mentor who will oversee his progress and preparation for final ordination. It is best if the mentor is already serving in a pastoral role in the candidate's church. If this is not available, the council may assign another willing and capable area pastor to serve as mentor. It is not recommended that a council member serve as a mentor unless he is willing to excuse himself from the council's examination of the man in the future.

The mentor plays an essential role in the candidate's pursuit of ordination. He assists the candidate in participating in a wide range of ministries during the years of Licensure, and serves as a link with the ordination council as the candidate progresses toward ordination. If, at any time, the candidate disqualifies himself from pastoral ministry, the mentor must communicate the situation to the council. The mentor is not a teacher so much as a supervisor whose purpose is to challenge the candidate to make the most of his years of Licensure, to observe his progress in ministry, and to give a final analysis to the council regarding the candidate's fitness for pastoral service.

Once a mentor has been assigned, the council member who has been charged with overseeing the candidate in question will set up ongoing communication with the mentor. In addition, the council member will send out additional Character Reference forms and Teaching Response forms to individuals who sit under the candidate's ministry for periodic appraisal of his character and gifts during this period of Licensure.

It is also important that, as the candidate participates in various areas of ministry during his years of Licensure, examples of his teaching and preaching be collected. Audio tapes of sermons and Bible studies, video copies of his teaching and preaching, along with written outlines, papers, or curricula originated by the candidate will allow the council to examine his gifts. Where possible, council members should take opportunity to hear a candidate preach or teach in person. Before the Second Ordination Examination it is important that council members have some understanding of the candidate's ability to minister the Word.

During the period of Licensure, the candidate will complete his Doctrinal Position Paper. Following its approval by his mentor, he will forward the paper to his assigned council member for a first reading. If it is approved without further suggestions, the council member will communicate to the Chairman that an acceptable paper has been received, and a date for the Second Ordination Examination can now be set. The paper will then be duplicated and sent, along with the most current Character Reference forms and Teaching Response forms, to the other council members for their study prior to the examination date.

The Second Ordination Examination

This final council examination represents the greatest opportunity both for the man and the church to determine the call of God on a man. It also can become a source of great encouragement to those candidates who demonstrate readiness in all areas. Because so much is at stake, this examination must be done well, in a manner that is both fair and thorough. As with the first examination, it is helpful to have the candidate bring his spouse, his pastor, his mentor, and some other godly acquaintances. As well, this examination should be open to all the church, for it provides an excellent opportunity to demonstrate the serious nature of the pastoral task, and can be a wonderful learning experience for all believers.

While various churches and denominations will handle this examination differently, here is a suggested model:

(1) Opening Instructions: Following a time of opening prayer and introductions, the council Chairman should overview the schedule for the day, and overview the procedure to be followed in examining the candidate. He should state the areas in which the candidate will be examined and briefly explain the scoring system. He should remind the candidate that the council expects answers to be clear, supported by Scripture, and a demonstration of the candidate's own study and thought. It should also be communicated to the candidate that he is free to ask a particular questioner for further explanation should he need it before answering, and that the council will consider that he is through with his answer when he stops talking and looks at the Chairman. Any special instructions for the council, audience, or candidate should be given at this time.

(2) Chairman's Charge: It is important that the Chairman sets the tone for the examination by declaring to the

audience and the candidate that they are about to embark on a very serious, yet wonderful task. He must make it clear that this is not an adversarial situation and that the council is not there to persecute the candidate! Rather, the council serves to promote the glory of God in protecting the ministry of the church and offer the candidate a thorough and thoughtful examination which, if completed successfully, will become to him an anchor of assurance that God has appointed him to pastoral ministry in the church.

(3) Council Questions: To ensure a complete examination, the council should follow a set design in its questions. It is best to begin with questions regarding the candidate's life (conversion, character, marriage, family, etc.) and then move to an examination of his knowledge. In assessing the candidate's theological, biblical, and pastoral knowledge it is helpful to follow the standard divisions of Systematic Theology beginning with Bibliology and progressing through to Eschatology. It is the Chairman's task to be sure that each section is covered sufficiently, and that each member of the council is afforded the opportunity to ask questions of the candidate before moving on to the next section. To facilitate this, it is often necessary for the council to create a list of questions or topics that must be covered in each section. Often this list of sample questions or topics will be part of the material given to the candidate in the Application Packet.

While the asking of questions is really an art, and each council member will adopt his own style, the following general suggestions will help the council obtain the type of information it needs to evaluate the candidate:

- Prepare your questions beforehand to be sure that what the question is asking is really what you want to know. Be sure it is clear, unambiguous, and specific.

- Be careful that in asking a question you do not give away the answer you are looking for. For example, I remember once a man asking the following: How do you understand the idea that Jesus voluntarily submitted the independent use of his divine attributes to the Father as a necessary part of becoming a man, as taught in Philippians 2:5-9? The very point of doctrine he was intending to discover was included in the question.

- Keep your questions specific and direct, and stay away from two - or three - part questions. It is best to ask one question, and then ask one or two follow-up questions, rather than ask a question with multiple parts which often end up being confusing to the candidate. Be sure that the candidate has finished before asking a follow-up question.

- Do your best to mask your viewpoint when asking controversial questions. Remember, you want to hear what the candidate thinks, and whether or not he can back it up. Giving too much of your own view may make him shy away from some particular area of his theology that he suspects is in opposition to yours.

- Stifle the urge to coach the candidate as he answers, or to help him if he seems hesitant or confused. If he needs further explanation, he is free to ask specific questions for further explanation. But don't rush to the rescue of a confused candidate! This is precisely what you are evaluating: his ability to think biblically and clearly, and to present his views with clarity and conviction.

- Ask questions that demand the use of Scripture. For example: How do you understand Psalm 2:7 in relation to the eternality of the Son?

- Lastly, be very careful not to show either disappointment or excitement over a candidate's answers.

(4) Questions to the mentor, spouse, and acquaintances: Following the public examination of the candidate, the council should dismiss the audience and the candidate, and spend some time with those people who have watched the man's progress over the past few years. This gives the council one last opportunity to hear reports regarding the candidate's character, ministry skills and gifts, and general fitness for ministry.

(5) Deliberation: Following the time of examination and questions, the council should spend time alone together discussing the candidate's answers and overall performance. During this time individual council members should rate the candidate using the scoring system. This will help the council determine its final decision.

(6) Communication: In a timely manner the Chairman should inform the candidate and his pastor of the council's decision. Where the candidate has been rejected the Chairman should be ready to give the council's concerns, along with their suggestions for the candidate's future progress.

The Ordination Service

After having completed the Second Ordination Examination successfully, the candidate is now ready to be publicly affirmed and appointed to pastoral ministry. Owing to the serious nature of the pastoral task, such a service ought to be a grand affair that includes the entire church family as well as those of neighboring churches. The purpose of the service will dictate its form. First, it is a service of thanksgiving to God for his provision of gifted men to the church. Music, the reading of Scripture, and prayer will all be appropriate. Secondly, it is a service of recognition, as the body of Christ gathers around a man whose divine appointment by God is affirmed through the laying on of hands. Thirdly, it is a service of responsibility as the candidate is reminded of the requirements God has for the pastoral office and task. It is here that several other pastors should be asked to address the candidate, reaffirming to him the specific standards of conduct and ministry set down by God. At this time the candidate should take public vows to remain faithful to his calling, his Lord, and the church. Lastly, it is a service of preaching as the newly ordained minister is allowed to open the Word of God and feed the people, declaring his heart for ministry through his exposition of the Word.

The Certificate of Ordination

The final task of the ordination council is to signify the candidate's ordained standing with an official document, signed by the council and the leaders of the candidate's church. Care should be taken to make this certificate something that will occupy an honored place in the life of the new minister. It should be first rate, nicely framed, and a credit to the diligent work of the man and the gracious provision of God.

Appendix

Gaining Knowledge and Discernment:
Suggested reading for those who preach, and those who want to.

In the first chapter of his epistle to the Philippians, the Apostle Paul reveals that at the core of his prayers for them is this: *that your love may abound still more and more in real knowledge and discernment, so that you may approve the things that are excellent ...* (1:9, 10a). What Paul desired for the Philippian church then is absolutely essential for ministers today. Every day they are confronted with numerous options for spending their time, responding to their world, dealing with sin and temptation, as well as protecting the sheep and proclaiming the truth.

Three dangers arise in this daily duel with the complexities of our world. First, a man may be weak and overwhelmed by all the choices facing him. Such a man most often fails because he fails to act, being paralyzed by his inability to make a firm decision. At the other end of the spectrum is the man who makes decisions freely, yet without consistent reasoning. This man comes to be regarded as inconsistent in his methods and capricious in his actions. Thirdly, there is the man who simply makes bad choices. All three of these leaders bring the consequences of their poor decision making down on their own heads, as well as on those who look to them and follow them. What our world and our churches need are men who, full of wisdom and knowledge, can make the right decisions, at the right time, for the right reasons. A. W. Tozer put it this way:

> The Church at this moment needs men, the right kind of men, bold men. The talk is that we need revival, that we need a new baptism of the Spirit – and God knows we must have both; but God will not revive mice. He will not fill rabbits with the Holy Ghost!

> We languish for men who feel themselves expendable in the warfare of the soul, who cannot be frightened by threats of death because they have already died to the allurements of this world. Such men will be free from the compulsions that control and squeeze weaker men.

> This kind of freedom is necessary if we are to have prophets in our pulpits again instead of mascots. These free men will serve God and mankind from motives too high to be understood by the rank and file of religious entertainers who today shuttle in and out of the sanctuary.

> They will make no decisions out of fear, take no course out of a desire to please, accept no service for financial considerations, perform no religious act out of mere custom; nor will they allow themselves to be influenced by the love of publicity or the desire for reputation.

> The true Church has never sounded out public expectations before launching her crusades. Her leaders heard from God, they knew their Lord's will and did it. Their people followed them – sometimes to triumph, oftener to insults and public persecution – and their sufficient reward was the satisfaction of being right in a wrong world! [1]

According to Tozer, the church languishes for men who can act freely and correctly in discerning God's will. According to Paul, the ability to do so is actually the

---

1   A. W. Tozer, *Renewed Day By Day*; edited by G. B. Smith; Christian Publications; Camp Hill, PA; 1989, August 11 reading.

fruit of real knowledge and discernment. A storehouse of knowledge trains the mind to see situations clearly, and moves the will to act courageously and righteously. For centuries, those who have been diligent to acquire knowledge and sharpen discernment have intentionally made it a life priority to read. Reading sharpens even as it fills; it exercises even as it refreshes. For those who would lead the church and preach the Word, not only must reading be a daily habit, but the scope of that reading must be both broad and deep.

For those considering the preaching ministry ...
Some of you who have read this book are in the process of determining if the desire you have to enter the preaching ministry is truly of God. The question of discernment begins for you with an examination of your internal call. Is the desire in your heart an indication that God intends you to serve as his appointed herald? While this book has given suggestions for answering that question, the following reading list in intended to help you further your pursuit of God's will.

Bearing in mind that knowledge is the foundation of discernment, you should consider the suggested reading list as a means of discovering just what the preaching office will demand of your character and dictate for your life. In testing the reality and sincerity of your desire (see: 1 Tim. 3:1) you must first have a clear understanding of what will be demanded of you should your desire be fulfilled. In many ways this can be compared to a young boy who, watching his father lather his face with shaving cream and remove the whiskers with the razor, is filled with a desire to start shaving as soon as possible. He daily checks the mirror for any indication that his beard is about to appear. But soon enough he will find that shaving holds no life-long pleasure. What he fantasized about as a boy all too soon becomes a daily chore that is, at best, inconvenient. In this case real knowledge of the activity brought clarity to his assessment. So it is with the ministry. As the stirrings of desire arise in your heart, you must test them against the reality of what God's man must be and do. The books that follow each give insight into the preacher's life and task. As you read, ask God that your desire for ministry would increase along with your knowledge of its rigors and rewards. If it does, you will have reason to believe that God is indeed drafting you into his royal service.

For those who occupy the preaching office ...
The following list of books are those that I have found to be particularly encouraging and beneficial in the day-to-day rigors of the preaching ministry. Some of them may already be old friends who occupy a place on your shelves and deserve a second reading. Others may be new to you and offer the chance to walk down a new path of learning. Either way I commend them to you with the prayer that your heart and mind will be enriched and your discernment heightened unto a more faithful and fruitful ministry for our Lord Christ.

A voice from the past with a challenge for today ...
John Wesley wrote the following to a fellow preacher, John Trembath, in 1760:

> What has exceedingly hurt you in time past, nay, and I fear to this day, is want of reading. I scarce ever knew a preacher read so little. And perhaps by neglecting it you have lost the taste for it. Hence your talent in preaching does not increase. It is just the same as it was seven years ago. It is lively, but not deep; there is little variety; there is no compass of thought; Reading only can supply this, with meditation and daily prayer. You wrong yourself greatly by omitting this. You can never be a deep preacher without it any more than a thorough Christian. O begin!

Fix some part of every day for private exercises. You may acquire the taste which you have not; what is tedious at first will afterwards be pleasant. Whether you like it or no; read and pray daily. It is for your life; there is no other way; else you will be a trifler all your days, and a pretty, superficial preacher.[2]

General Reading:
These works are good general overviews of the pastoral office and task.

1. Patrick Fairbairn, *Pastoral Theology*; Reprinted by Old Paths Publications; Audubon, New Jersey; 1992. Subtitled 'A Treatise on the Office and Duties of the Christian Pastor', this book is a gem, and has an especially good section on the administration of church discipline.

2. J. I. Packer, *A Quest for Godliness*; Crossway Books; Wheaton, IL; 1990. Subtitled 'The Puritan Vision of the Christian Life', this book is an excellent treatment of the essential characteristics and themes that made up the life and ministries of the Puritans. The sections of puritan family life and preaching are very helpful.

3. C.H. Spurgeon, *Lectures to My Students*, Christian Focus Publications, Scotland, 1997. What C.H. Spurgeon wanted his ministerial students to know makes for good reading and reflection today.

4. John Calvin, *Institutes of the Christian Religion* (in 2 volumes); edited by John T. McNeill; translated by Ford Lewis Battles; The Westminster Press; Philadelphia, 1945. The grand treatise on Christian doctrine by one of the finest theologians ever is also one of the

---

2   John Wesley, *The Message of the Wesleys*, edited by Philip S. Watson; MacMillian.

best places to read about the pastoral office. Calvin, himself first and foremost a pastor, brings great insight and biblical wisdom to the areas of the pastoral call and ordination, as well as the demands and tasks of the pastoral office.

5. John MacArthur, Jr., editor; *Rediscovering Pastoral Ministry*; Word Publishing; Dallas; 1995. This collection of essays by Master's Seminary professors includes excellent material on all major aspects of pastoral ministry including the call to ministry, preparation for ministry, the minister's personal life and home, and the wide range of ministerial tasks.

Pastoral Ministry:

1. Thomas C. Oden, *Classical Pastoral Care* (in four volumes); Baker Books; Grand Rapids; 1987. This four volume set offers the views of ancient Christian pastoral writers on numerous subjects relating to the pastoral office. The individual volumes are entitled *Becoming a Minister, Ministry through Word and Sacrament, Pastoral Counsel,* and *Crisis Ministries.*

2. Peter White, *The Effective Pastor*, Christian Focus Publications, Scotland; 1998. This is a book for trainee ministers, new ministers and experienced ministers alike. Sinclair Ferguson says of this book that 'there has long been a need for a contemporary manual of biblical and practical instruction on the work of the ministry. *The Effective Pastor* recognises this need and meets it. It will be widely welcomed, eagerly read and should stimulate thought and discussion.'

3. John MacArthur, Jr., *Shepherdology*, The Master's Fellowship; Panorama City, CA; 1989. Subtitled 'A Master Plan for Church Leadership'.

4. John R. W. Stott, *The Preacher's Portrait*, Eerdmans; Grand Rapids; 1961. This book studies the various titles given to the minister in the New Testament and gives the implications of each.

5. T. W. Manson, *The Servant-Messiah*, Baker Books; Grand Rapids; 1977. This study of the public ministry of Christ is helpful for those who would minister as His heralds.

6. Ronald S. Wallace, *Calvin's Doctrine of the Word & Sacrament*, Eerdmans; Grand Rapids; 1957. Even those not ministering in the Reformed tradition will find the pastoral aspects of this book of great benefit.

Preaching:
That preaching is the primary task of God's herald is self evident. These books offer insight, both broad and deep, of what is involved in preaching, and in remaining qualified as a preacher.

1. Samuel T. Logan, ed., *The Preacher and Preaching*, P & R Publishing; Phillipsburg, NJ. Subtitled 'Reviving the Art in the Twentieth Century' this collection of essays by well known pastors and scholars in the Reformed tradition is very helpful. J.I. Packer's Introduction entitled 'Why Preach' is exceptional.

2. Arturo G. Azurdia III, *Spirit Empowered Preaching*, Christian Focus Publications, Scotland; 1998. A response to one of the great dangers that face today's preachers, the problem of an over intellectual approach to preaching. Careful, meditative and painstaking exegesis brings a potential liability, that of losing the vitality which must accompany exposition. The author points out the importance of pastors obtaining power from God as well as gaining insight into the subjects about which they preach.

3. R. Bruce Bickel, *Light and Heat: The Puritan View of the Pulpit*, Soli Deo Gloria; Morgan, PA; 1999. This excellent little book focuses both on the puritan view of preaching, and their use of the gospel in preaching.

4. D. Martyn Lloyd-Jones, *Preaching and Preachers*, Zondervan; Grand Rapids; 1972. Don't even think about preaching until you read this book.

5. John Piper, *The Supremacy of God in Preaching*, Baker Books, Grand Rapids; 1990. A necessary book by one of today's leading American preachers.

6. E. M. Bounds, *Powerful and Prayerful Pulpits*, edited by Darrel D. King, Baker Books, Grand Rapids; 1993. This collection of material from E. M. Bounds is organized into forty daily readings on the subject of the preacher and his tasks. Taken together, these short essays walk the reader through a host of practical themes and reflections on anointed ministry.

7. Robert L. Reymond, *Preach the Word!*, Rutherford House; Edinburgh; 1988. This book is dedicated to 'all those faithful preachers who are committed to a theologically articulate ministry in which the whole counsel of God is proclaimed with power and with proportion but without apology'. Think of the kind of book that would lay a simple, yet profound foundation for such a ministry, and you have this one. Hard to find, but well worth the effort.

8. William Perkins, *The Art of Prophesying*, The Banner of Truth Trust; Edinburgh; 1996. This puritan preacher carefully studies the fundamental aspects of preaching (termed 'prophesying' in his day) in customary puritan warmth and completeness.

9. Dave Eby, *Power Preaching*, Christian Focus Publications, Scotland; 1996. Considers the role of preaching in growing churches, particularly in response to the emphasis of the church growth movement which has not given preaching the priority the New Testament gives to it.

10. Philips Brooks, *Lectures on Preaching*, Baker Books, Grand Rapids; 1969. These lectures, originally given at Yale in 1877, offer insights into the preacher and preaching by the man best known for defining preaching as 'truth through personality'.

11. David Jackman (editor), *Preaching the Living Word*, Christian Focus Publications, Scotland; 1999. This is a collection of addresses given at the Evangelical Ministry Assembly, held annually in London in July. J I Packer deals with perspectives on preaching, Bruce Milne explains preaching hell and preaching heaven, Alec Motyer deals with preaching the Old Testament, Mark Ashton explores the role of preaching in building a congregation, and Peter Jensen discusses the contribution preaching has to faith.

12. T. H. L. Parker, *Calvin's Preaching*, Westminster/John Knox Press, Louisville, KY; 1992. Written by one of today's foremost scholars on Calvin, this book is a masterful manual on preaching readily useable for today's pulpits. And as a bonus, the reader is presented with an intimate portrait of John Calvin as the pastor and preacher.

13. Gardiner Spring, *The Power of the Pulpit*, The Banner of Truth Trust; Edinburgh; 1986. Dr Spring should be listened to if for no other reason than he pastored the same church for 62 years. This book stresses ministerial diligence, competence, education, and responsibility.

It ends with a delightful and sobering essay on 'The Responsibility of Enjoying the Christian Ministry'.

14. Tony Sargent, *The Sacred Annointing*, Crossway Books, Wheaton; 1994. This book studies the preaching of Dr David Martyn Lloyd-Jones and offers insight both into the man and his extraordinary pulpit ministry.

15. James Philip, *Recovering the Word,* Fellowship of Word and Spirit, Hartford, Northwich, England; 1993. This small booklet speaks to the need for expository preaching today. Exceptional!

16. A. N. Martin, *What's Wrong with Preaching Today?,* The Banner of Truth Trust; Edinburgh; 1992. While giving reasons for today's decline in preaching, Pastor Martin gives a biblical portrait of what God's preacher looks like, and what he does in the pulpit.

Personal Life:

The personal life of the minister is a thing of great concern to Christ. As Paul points out in his letter to Timothy and Titus, a man's character and spiritual maturity form the foundation of his usefulness. These books will give you encouragement to pursue godly character and habits daily, and for your lifetime.

1. Horatius Bonar, *Words to Winners of Souls*, Hegg Bros Printing, Tacoma, WA; 1971. This small booklet is a must read for any aspiring or practicing minister of the gospel. It regularly goes in and out of print so buy several when you can. You will find, after reading it, that you are driven to give one to every minister you know.

2. D. A Carson, *A Call to Spiritual Reformation*, Baker Books, Grand Rapids, MI; 1996. Dr Carson challenges the reader to adopt the set of spiritual priorities set forth in the prayers of the Apostle Paul.

3. Donald S. Whitney, *Spiritual Disciplines for the Christian Life*, NavPress, Colorado Springs, CO; 1994. A very insightful and useable manual covering the necessary spiritual habits of Bible intake, prayer, meditation, journaling, etc.

4. John H. Armstrong; *The Stain that Stays*, Christian Focus, Scotland; 2000. Subtitled 'The church's response to sexual misconduct' this book tackles the whole subject of ministerial disqualification.

5. Donald Bloesch, *The Struggle of Prayer*, Helmers & Howard, Colorado Springs, CO; 1988. Anyone honest enough to admit that prayer is a struggle deserves to be heard. Dr Bloesch goes deeply into the necessity of restoring Biblical prayer.

6. O. Hallesby, *Prayer*, Augsburg, Minneapolis; 1994. Written by one of Norway's leading teachers and devotional writers, this book gives the insights on prayer from an author who was imprisoned for his resistance to the Nazi regime during World War II.

7. John Bunyan, *The Fear of God*, Reprinted by Soli Deo Gloria, Morgan, PA; 1999. Ministry for God rises first from a righteous fear of God. This classic treatment of an essential subject has been reprinted with many helpful spelling, format, and grammar changes.

8. Eugene Peterson, *The Contemplative Pastor*, Eerdmans, Grand Rapids; 1989. This book will make you think in ways – and about things – you probably have never thought before. Do it anyway and you will be richer for the experience.

9. Dr and Mrs Howard Taylor, *Hudson Taylor's Spiritual Secret*, China Inland Mission; London, 1935. This book

will help you understand the ministerial privilege of total dependence upon God.

10. Richard A. Swenson, *Margin*, NavPress, Colorado Springs, CO; 1992. Written by a Christian physician, this book aims to help the reader 'restore emotional, physical, financial, and time reserves' to overloaded lives. While not written specifically for those in ministry, any minister without 'margin' in his life will be neither successful nor long-lasting.

Doctrine:
For those beginning their theological instruction, or looking for useable reference works as resources for theological papers, the following books provide a starting point.

1. William Cunningham, *Historical Theology* (in two volumes), Reprinted by Still Waters Revival Books, Edmonton, Canada; 1991. First published in 1882, this set gives an excellent review of 'the principal doctrinal discussions in the Christian Church since the Apostolic Age'.

2. Wayne Grudem, *Systematic Theology*, Zondervan, Grand Rapids; 1994. A very readable and complete discussion of the various sections of systematic theology. Excellent!

3. J. I. Packer, *Concise Theology*, Tyndale, Wheaton; 1993. Dr Packer consistently says more in less space than most other theologians. This book is the best example as he clearly describes, defines and defends 94 theological concepts – all in three pages or less.

4. R. K. McGregor Wright, *No Place for Sovereignty*, InterVarsity Press, Downers Grove, IL., 1996. Subtitled 'What's Wrong With Freewill Theism' this book is

theology for the tough minded. But those who make the effort will be rewarded with the best treatment of why the sovereignty of God in the salvation of God is a non-negotiable item if a minister is to be faithful to the Word of God.

Contemporary Issues:

Knowing how the ministry demands that a man defends the truth and withstands the inroads of culture, I offer the following books both as an opportunity to consider issues now facing the church, and as models of the critical thinking necessary to 'exhort in sound doctrine and to refute those who contradict' (Titus 1:9).

1. Michael Scott Horton, editor, *Power Religion*, Moody Press, Chicago; 1992. Several leading biblical scholars and preachers discuss the difference between society's strategies for power and the biblical patterns.

2. John H. Armstrong, editor, *The Coming Evangelical Crisis*, Moody Press, Chicago; 1996. A fine collection of church leaders and educators offer essays on areas of theology and church life where the evangelical church is currently at risk.

3. John H. Armstrong, editor, *The Compromised Church*, Crossway Books, Wheaton; 1998. In surveying areas where the church has been influenced by culture, the authors of these essays present ways to regain ecclesiastical obedience.

4. G. A Pritchard, *Willow Creek Seeker Services*, Baker Books, Grand Rapids; 1996. The evangelical world has been overwhelmed with a philosophy of church ministry driven to attract and retain the unchurched 'seeker'. This philosophy has caused so many to change so much of what once was considered the right way to 'do church'.

This book represents a three year doctoral research project on the flagship church in the 'seeker driven' community. The critique is both balanced and searing.

5. David Peterson, *Engaging with God*, Eerdmans; Grand Rapids; 1992. Subtitled 'A Biblical Theology of Worship' this is simply, the best book on the subject ever.

6. Andreas J. Kostenberger, et al, editors; *Women in the Church*, Baker Books, Grand Rapids; 1995. This book deals with 1 Timothy 2:9-15 and supports the complementarian view of the role of women in the church.

7. Kenneth Prior, The *Gospel in a Pagan Society*, Christian Focus Publications, Scotland; 1995. Considers the vital question of how we communicate the Gospel in a non-Christian society. Kenneth Prior takes lessons from the example of the Apostle Paul who faced the same problems in Athens nearly 2,000 years ago. Highly motivated, he was willing to go over to where the pre-Christians were, to speak to them in language they understood, reaching them at the point of need; but his message was also clear and uncompromising, not sacrificing any aspect of Christian truth.

Scripture Index

Exodus
3:9................18
3:10................18

Numbers
27: 12-23.......18

Joshua
1:1-9.............19

Ezra
7:6-10............85

Psalms
2:7................139

Isaiah
6:1-5.............19
6:6................19
6:9................19

Jeremiah
1:5................19
1:6................19
1:7................20
1:9................20
1:17-19..........20

Ezekiel
1–3................20
34.................50

Jonah
1:2................20
3:2................20
3:5................19

Malachi
3:1-5.............50
3:11................50

Matthew
6:19-21..........87

Mark
1:4................27
1:14................27
1:38................27

Luke
1:19................29
2:10-12..........30
14:28..............96
24:32..............83

John
3:22-36..........72
13:16..............96

Acts
6:3................40
8:4................27
13:2................37
13:3................37
14.................24
14:23........33, 40
15:40..............38
17:2-4.............83
20:17-28.........34
20:28..............67

Romans
1:16..........47, 64
10:14-15.........28
12:17..............88
12:21..............88

1 Corinthians
1:17................47
1:18................64
1:21................47
1:24................64
11:1................57

2 Corinthians
2:14–4:7.........63
2:14-16..........63
3:4-6.........63, 94
4:1-10.............72
4:7................63
5:18................58
5:19..............114
10:5-7............64

Galatians
1–2................36
2:1-10..........125
2:1................37
2:2................37
2:9................37
3:28..............114
6:1................88
6:14................74

Ephesians
4:1-16............49

4:11-13..........34
4:11-16....44, 49

Philippians
1:9-11............85
2:5-9............138

Colossians
1:24................70

1 Timothy
1:3-5..............26
1:3...........26, 38
1:18-20..........26
1:18-19..........62
2:7................26
2:12-13........114
3 ....97, 132
3:1-13.............26
3:1-8................41
3:1-7 ...50, 55, 59
3:1ff................29
3:1..........29, 67,
...........68, 143
3:2................81
3:4-5..............84
3:7................40
3:8-13..............33
3:15................26
3:16-17........115
4:6................26
4:7................26
4:11................26
4:12.........26, 62
4:13................26
4:14....26, 28, 38,
.........39, 125
4:16..........26, 65,
................110
5:21................26
6:3-19............87
6:11................26
6:12-14..........26
6:14................39
6:17-18..........26
6:20-21..........39

2 Timothy
1:5................61
1:6-14......61, 70

1:6.....26, 28, 39,
61, 62, 63, 125
1:7......62, 63, 86
1:8............66, 70
1:11..........26, 28
1:12................70
1:13-14..........26
2:2......40, 50, 56
2:2-6.............62
2:15................26
2:17................50
2:19-22..........26
2:24-26....26, 50
2:24-25.77, 81, 88
3:14-16..........26
3:14..........62, 77
3:17................64
4:1-5........27, 50
4:1-4............125
4:2............27, 38
4:5................62
4:6-8................61
4:15................26

Titus
1 97
1:5-9........26, 55
1:6-9 ...41, 50, 59
1:6................84
1:9............77, 81
2:11-14..........26
2:15....48, 83, 85
3:8................85

Hebrews
12:15..............88

1 Peter
5:1-3.............59
5:2................84
5:3................84

2 Peter
2:1................50
2:5................26

1 John
2:2................114

Jude
1-4.................50

155

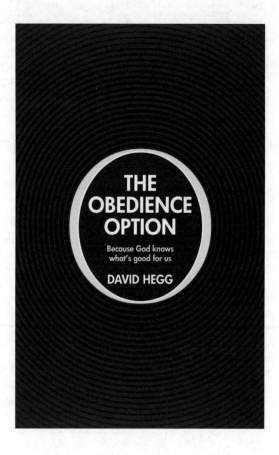

THE
OBEDIENCE
OPTION

Because God knows
what's good for us

DAVID HEGG

The Obedience Option
DAVID HEGG

The Obedience Option guides Christ followers through the book of Ephesians in the pursuit of an "overwhelming faith" — a life-dominating conviction that all God has for us through obedience is better by far than anything Satan can offer through selfishness and sin. In this state a passion for righteousness overwhelms other passions. Righteous living becomes our joy and God's purposes are achieved in our lives. Christ is displayed consistently and conspicuously to a world in need.

David Hegg has written this very helpful book to show why obedience to God is always the best of all our choices. Carefully, skillfully tracing the theme through several passages of Scripture, he shows why obedience is not merely our duty; it can also be our delight.

JOHN MACARTHUR,
Pastor, Grace Community Church, Sun Valley, California

Written by a veteran pastor, this well-informed book encourages and challenges us to think about crucial truths at the intersection of faith and practice.

MICHAEL HORTON,
J. Gresham Machen Professor of Systematic Theology and Apologetics,
Westminster Seminary California

Sin is serious. But you can forsake it. Let David Hegg show you why obeying God is better by far than indulging the flesh.

COLLIN HANSEN,
editorial director, The Gospel Coalition;
co-author, 'A God-Sized Vision: Revival Stories That Stretch and Stir'

ISBN 978-1-84550-606-3

GREG SCHARF

PREPARED TO PREACH

GOD'S WORK & OURS IN PROCLAIMING HIS WORD

Prepared to Preach
Greg Scharf

Prepared to Preach offers an accessible and concise aid for all those who have been challenged to preach or feel a growing compulsion to do so. This is an essential read for all those who are wondering precisely where to start in preparing to expound God's word, whether it is for the Divinity Student, the layperson, the parachurch worker or the short-term missionary. This is a comprehensive yet digestible guide. Scharf focuses on the attitudes and skills those inexperienced in preaching need to develop, whilst at all times re-enforcing that although there are a number of things you, the preacher, must do, it is what God does that is at the heart of preaching. This book illuminates to us how to prepare our minds to preach, how to prepare the congregation to hear and obey God's word, how to prepare the message God gives you to preach, and also how to deliver the message you have prepared.

Throughout it all, Scharf is motivated by a tremendous concern to equip preachers so that they might clearly express God's word.

Greg Scharf is Associate Professor and Chair of the department of Pastoral Theology at Trinity Evangelical Divinity School in Deerfield, Illinois. He has served as president of the Evangelical Homiletics Society and is married with three sons, two daughters-in-law and one granddaughter.

ISBN 978-1-84550-043-6

Christian Focus Publications
publishes books for all ages

Our mission statement –

STAYING FAITHFUL
In dependence upon God we seek to impact the world through literature faithful to His infallible Word, the Bible. Our aim is to ensure that the LORD Jesus Christ is presented as the only hope to obtain forgiveness of sin, live a useful life and look forward to heaven with Him.

REACHING OUT
Christ's last command requires us to reach out to our world with His gospel. We seek to help fulfil that by publishing books that point people towards Jesus and help them develop a Christ-like maturity. We aim to equip all levels of readers for life, work, ministry and mission.

Books in our adult range are published in three imprints.
Christian Focus contains popular works including biographies, commentaries, basic doctrine and Christian living. Our children's books are also published in this imprint.
Mentor focuses on books written at a level suitable for Bible College and seminary students, pastors, and other serious readers. The imprint includes commentaries, doctrinal studies, examination of current issues and church history.
Christian Heritage contains classic writings from the past.

Christian Focus Publications Ltd,
Geanies House, Fearn, Ross-shire,
IV20 1TW, Scotland, United Kingdom
info@christianfocus.com
www.christianfocus.com